NORTHWOOD'S NATURALIST

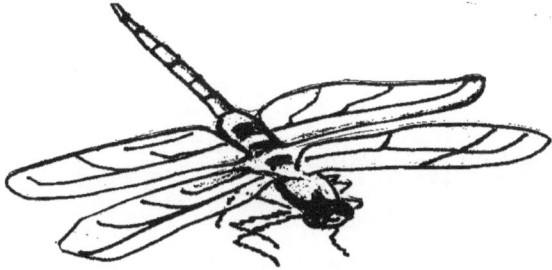

DAVE PAULSON

F Frog
Productions

ISBN 978-0-6151-5430-5

Artwork by Dave Paulson, except illustrations on pages ii, 13, 16, 17, & 54 courtesy of Ryan Kelly

First Printing 2007

F Frog
Productions
5237 County Road A
Webster, WI 54893
(715) 866-8816

For the love of nature, The Creator, & Renae,
without which this would not be possible.

Thanks to everyone that has expressed support,
encouragement, and appreciation for what
began as a little newsletter and has
blossomed into so much more.

See you on the trail!

Contents

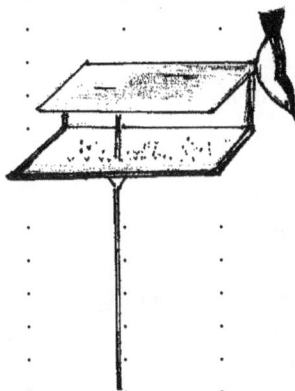

INTRODUCTION

Often people I meet will ask me what I do. While I can tell them my place of employment and trivial details about a job, it does not truly answer the question. What I do is more appropriately answered in what I am. What I am is a connoisseur of nature, or simply – a naturalist.

People wrestle with that answer. A naturalist? Oh, a forester, or tree-hugger, a biologist, or camper they say. So, what is a naturalist? Ask 10 folks and get 10 different answers. For me, it is a way to look at the world, to interact with nature, to discover, learn, and enjoy the natural world around me, and then to share that with others. To be able to give simple answers to questions about what owl you saw in your backyard, where frogs go in the winter, and which flowers are currently in bloom, and then go on to the deeper truths about why it is there, what it is doing, and its relationship within the environment.

This journey is lifelong - full of simple joys (a chickadee in January), complex relationships (the local water shed), and reoccurring visits (the spring flowers on the forest floor). One never graduates. Sure, there are learning curves, like the first attempt to successfully identify a warbler, waiting for a butterfly to land then realizing there's no film in the camera, and coming back from a hike with more questions than answers, but the journey is the reward.

Folks say that when you find your calling in life it is consuming labor of love. It cries out to be fed and released like the soaking up and wringing out of a sponge. Through writing and teaching I have been able to celebrate the creations of this earth and recognize the grace and wisdom found in nature. To acknowledge the God of all things and find His peace in things wild. To see glory in the trees, blessings in the birds, and splendor in the wildlife that surrounds us. The desire to share my passion, observations, and experiences for the place I call home is in the hope that you'll see the wonder and witness the magic of your own "backyard."

The essays serve as a touchstone and provide both the simple answers and greater truths about the natural history in northern Wisconsin and throughout the Upper Midwest. More importantly, we need to get out in the woods and experience nature firsthand. Its fun to identify plants and trees, recognize birds by their song, and collect a lifetime of wildlife memories. Furthermore, seeing the connection and role that the natural resource has within the environment is paramount to truly understanding nature and making wise choices in our daily lives. Take time to bask in the natural world and your senses will come alive, your knowledge and appreciation will abound, and you will find peace and wonderment contrary to anything else this man-made life can give.

You will go out in joy and be led forth
in peace; the mountains and hills will
burst forth into song before you, and all
of the trees of the field will clap their hands.
Isaiah 55:12

WINTER

If we slow down, take time to listen, and
commit oneself to learning the ways of nature,
we will know true wisdom.

Winter Wonderland

Winter is upon us and we wait with great anticipation to see what weather befalls us. A cold and snowy forecast is the early season prediction, but that has yet to come to fruition. Past years have seen some of the warmest Januarys on record. I think deep down many folks like to see a hearty winter, with blankets of snow and enough cold nights to test the car battery. For us in the upper midwest, a tough winter is our badge of fortitude we wear proudly, a testament to the tenacity with which we face the season, and our touchstone to times past when snow drifts enshrouded the house, brought traffic to a standstill, and gathered children of all ages to the local sledding hill.

Often it is hard to believe that much activity can be taking place out in the forest. At first glance, the woods may appear desolate and barren, from standing on the edge peering in. Upon closer inspection and after a few footsteps, evidence will present itself to the contrary. Fox tracks may appear as the time has come to go in search of a mate. Piles of tan, fibrous jellybeans can be found at the base of hollow pine trees, indicating the inhabitant of a porcupine and its signature scat pile. Bushes and saplings are gnawed at the base and large prints that trail into the underbrush signal the snowshoe hare's activity. And of course, our feathered friends add color and harmony as we trek across the landscape. Nuthatches, chickadees, blue jays, brown creepers, and woodpeckers are keeping busy as they prepare to raise another family. Somewhere a bat, bear, and mourning cloak butterfly are nestled away for the next three months – but even from a bear's slumber, new life will emerge in the form of bear cubs born in late January or February. These are busy times for the wildlife.

One of the first birds to pair up and prepare their nest is the great horned owl. While not exactly a guest at the backyard feeder, the great horned owl, *Bubo virginianus*, may be closer than you think. This owl is at home in a variety of habitats and is considered one of the great hunters in the wildlife kingdom. Some folks call them "flying tigers" because of their voracious appetite and hunting prowess.

Primarily nocturnal hunters, owls have exceptionally keen eyesight, fringed wing feathers enabling then to fly silently, and acute hearing making them efficient predators. Great horned owls will attack and kill most anything it can carry off, including rabbits, small rodents, frogs, snakes, cats, and other owls. Because they lack a strong sense of smell, great horns are the only real natural predator of skunks.

Great horned owls and all owls belong to a group of birds called raptors. Other raptors include hawks, osprey, and eagles. All raptors have a curved beak, sharp talons used for grasping their

3

prey, and are carnivorous. Interestingly, raptors do not drink water as songbirds do, but rather obtain liquids directly from the food they eat.

Beginning in January, great horned owls establish territories and begin nesting. Pairs will not build nests but instead take over an unoccupied raven or hawk nest. Females typically lay two or three eggs, hatching 30 days later in early March. The owlets are born blind and featherless. Their survival is a testament to the parenting skills of the great horned owl. During the coldest time of the year, the hatchlings will grow and eventually leave the nest to stake their own claim in nature.

At home in forests, deserts, swamps, and city parks, great horned owls continue to thrive because of their varied diet and hunting skills. Look for the brownish gray feathers, large ear tuffs (hence the name "horned"), and large yellow eyes that distinguish this owl. Listen for their resounding hoots when out for a late night stroll. These elusive, nocturnal "tigers of the sky" may indeed be wise after all.

On the Tail's Trail

Winter is a great time to learn or test your tracking skills. The eastern cottontail is a great animal to start with. This small rabbit has the familiar brown/gray coat and a whitish gray rump patch. Cottontails generally reside in brushy fields or woodlots and during the winter months will often seek shelter under the porch or deck of your house.

After a snowfall, look for two oval tracks with two smaller tracks behind and closer together. The two larger tracks are the hind feet landing in front of the rabbit, with the two shorter front feet landing in back. As children, many of us did this awkward stride in gym class during relay races. The larger back feet allow the cottontail to move at speeds topping out at 18 miles per hour. Look for tracks around shrubs and woody vegetation they may be browsing on or under backyard bird feeders.

Small symmetrical droppings are another tell-tale sign of the eastern cottontail. These small balls of scat are tan and sometimes green in color and contain fibrous material. I often find, seemingly hundreds of these dropping around my feeder during the week. Thankfully the fresh snowfall covers them up! Cottontails are considered crepuscular animals, meaning that they are most active during the hours around dusk and dawn. After the next snowfall, check around for tracks that may lead you to their resting place. Good luck and goodwill tracking.

Simple Pleasures of the Balsam Fir

The northwood's only fir tree can easily go unnoticed eleven months out of the year. Then in December, it becomes everyone's favorite Christmas tree, harvested for millions of homes throughout the country. This ubiquitous tree of the north can also provide shelter, health, and medical benefits too.

The balsam fir is an evergreen tree, also called a conifer because it bears cones. The branches grow in whorls from the center trunk. The outer branches split into three parts, all carrying the needle-like leaves. Balsam fir needles are flat and blunt and if you turn a needle over, you will see two parallel, white "racing" stripes. Confusion between a fir and a spruce tree is easily remedied by placing a needle between your thumb and index finger. Try rolling the needle against your thumb. Spruce needles will roll, balsam needles will not.

The balsam fir is perfect for the accumulating snow in the north. The flexible branches will simply fold downwards when the snow load gets too heavy. Go for a hike after a heavy snow and you can hear the snow slipping off the trees and watch the branches spring back as if giving you a little wave. Looking closely at the trunk will reveal small blisters. These blisters contain resin that smell so fresh and aromatic, yet are very sticky to touch. The resin is used as clear glue for optical lenses and microscope slides. The resin can also be put over small cuts – a natural band-aid if you will.

Animals will use balsam fir as thermal cover in the winter - nesting under the branches, and a few animals such as the hare, will browse the twigs. Balsam fir makes great tea and stuffing your pillow with balsam boughs is thought to be a remedy for the cough. The logging industry harvests the tree for pulpwood, and although not widely reported - this tree can also provide lots of wilderness entertainment too.

While leading a group of students through the Sylvania Wilderness, in the Upper Peninsula of Michigan, I watched as one student hurried ahead to the nearest balsam fir tree flocked with snow. He would nestle in tight to the trunk, give it a gentle shake, and laugh as the snow came showering down upon him. I also had a college professor that introduced us to "balsam boat races." He popped one of the resin blisters and carefully coated the ends of two small twigs with the gooey substance. Then he gently placed them in a standing pool of water. We watched as the resin and water repelled each other sending the two twigs off to the races. The resin left an "oil slick" on the water's surface. You can't buy entertainment this good!

Balsam fir provides us with year-round color and quietly adds to our quality of life. The winter landscape is textured and aesthetically pleasing because of this conifer. Take time to stop and discover the simple pleasures of the balsam fir.

Talkin' Turkey

Turkeys have historically been a part of southern Wisconsin, thriving in the oak woodlands and rolling topography of the area, and during the winter of 2004, turkeys were introduced into the northwoods.

The Eastern Wild Turkey, *Mileagris galopavo silvistris*, is typically found amongst mast producing trees such as oak and hickory, which are staples of their diet. But turkeys are opportunistic and

7

will feed also on grains, seeds, and the soft mast from hawthorns, high bush cranberry, June berry, rose hips, hazel, and mountain ash. Several local chapters of the National Wild Turkey Federation trapped birds from Langlade County and released them into parts of Douglas and Bayfield Counties in March, 2004. These areas have rolling topography with both pin and burr scrub oak, along with the aforementioned soft mast producing plants. A total of 75 turkeys were released to provide hunting opportunities and bird watching experiences for the public, as the spring courtship displays are impressive to watch.

Over the past several years turkeys have expanded their range and are common sights along the fields and roadways of northwestern Wisconsin. Turkeys can survive the cold winter as long as food is available, but have to elude predators such as the coyote, bobcat, and great horned owl. After the next snowfall, go for a turkey trot and try to follow their oversized bird tracks while listening for gobbles, rustling feathers, and groups searching for food. Red pine plantations are common roosting habitats for these gregarious fowl friends, so that's a good place to start. And that's no jive!

The Daily Planner

As a way to keep organized and not to forget important meetings, many folks carry a daily planner, palm pilot, pocket organizer, have a desk calendar, or attach post-it notes everywhere. We are driven by time and often see our day as a reflection of accomplishments. What about wildlife? They do not have calendars, schedules, or appointments to keep. How do the birds and animals know when it is time to mate, build nests, defend territory, migrate, or forage for food? Part of the answer lies in phenology.

Phenology is the study of relationships between climate and recurring natural events in nature. The seasons drive many of the behaviors in the wild, and the amount of daylight, along with the angle of the sun, triggers migratory and hibernation activity. Throw in instincts and hormones, and the answer is complete. This explains why the majority of mammals in the northwoods mate during the winter months. After a typical 45-90 day gestation, the young are born in late spring with adequate food sources and ample vegetation for cover.

While the average person does not witness mating behaviors, we can take the word of experts and rely on past research for such information. However, we can record our own phenology observations when it comes to bird behavior and plant life. Have you noticed the birds lately? Are the male chickadees singing their territorial and mating call *"fe be, fe bebe,"* and are the cardinals more vocal these days? Look for and note sightings of redpolls and snowy owls this time of year. Examine the buds on different trees, especially the red maples. And watch the constellations as they shift into their winter alignment.

Winter is a wonderful season with so much to see and do. The landscape takes on a new personality after a wet snowfall. The night sky is clearer (cold air holds less water vapor than warm air) and the stars dance with a brighter twinkle. Wildlife leave footprints in the snow and we can follow their trail and imagine what they are up to. Keep track of what you see and hear, and then pretty soon you'll be talking like an "old timer," telling stories about winters past and predictions of winters to come.

A Cure for the Common Cold?

I often hear complaints regarding the length and temperature of winter. It's too long, too cold, and there is not enough sunlight, some folks say. Reports indicate that some people suffer a light deprived depression during this season. While I am not a doctor, I would like to prescribe my homemade remedy for a case of the winter blues: an hour with nature's cheeriest resident – the black capped chickadee.

Take a walk through your neighborhood park or along a mixed forest trail, with lots of aspen, birch, and pine trees. Listen for the familiar call "*de de de, de de de,*" and watch for flying "cotton balls" flitting through the trees. Once spotted, try repeating the sound "pish" over thirty seconds. Chickadees are notoriously tame and curious. Often the birds will fly in close to investigate the sound. With a bit of patience and an outstretched handful of birdseed, you may entice one to land for a snack. They always put a smile on my face as they tip their heads and look inquisitively at me.

Chickadees are year-round residents and typically live in flocks of 6-10 birds. They keep company with nuthatches, creepers, downy woodpeckers, and kinglets. The strong silent types they are not. If fact, black capped chickadees are quite vocal, and constantly communicate within the flock. Two common calls are the *"tset"* and *"de de de"* used to keep in touch with others and share food locations.

Chickadees weigh less than an ounce, but have an internal body temperature between 104-109° Fahrenheit. Besides fluffing out their feathers to trap air for insulation, chickadees begin shivering to increase metabolism and generate heat. At night they roost in conifer trees or cavities in birch trees and are able to lower their body temperature to conserve heat and stay warm.

Backyard feeders come alive with chickadees during the winter. Besides black oil sunflower seeds, they eat conifer seeds, berries, sap, and search the trees for hidden insect larvae. A person cannot help but be drawn into their carefree world of winter frolic and feeding. These mini-acrobats are sure to warm the soul of anyone feeling down and brighten up even the cloudiest day.

Romance in the Forest

Before I became a naturalist, I never paid much attention to Valentine's Day. Probably because I always seemed to find myself in the lonely hearts club band playing first chair. Thankfully, things have changed – not only in my social life but also in my perspective of the natural world. Nowadays, Valentine's Day serves as a reminder to me that there is a lot going on in the woods this time of year, namely, romance amongst the critters. However, let us back up a bit.

Some of you might be wondering where the origin of Valentine's Day came from? The Roman Catholic Church recognizes several Saint Valentines. One popular story follows the life of a priest named Valentine, serving in Rome under the reign of Emperor Claudius II. Seems Claudius, wanting to strengthen his army, forbid marriage among young men. Valentine ignored this decree and secretly married young couples in an underground church. This lead to Valentine's arrest and imprisonment, where as legend has it, he sent out letters to the jailer's daughter – signed "your Valentine." Valentine's death was said to be on Feb. 14. Another inspiration for Valentine's Day comes from the European belief that birds began mating on February 14. Authors such as Shakespeare and Chaucer commonly wrote about this. With that in mind, let's look at what's going on today.

It makes sense that many animals would start their mating season now. Following mating and a one or two month gestation, the young will be born soon after spring has started, when food should be plentiful and the opportunity to learn the ways of their species will be ideal. One of the first to mate in the wild is the great horned owl. Great horn owls pair up early and start mating in January. After laying several eggs, the owlets are hatched 30 days later. Great horned owls, considered excellent parents, will fiercely defend the nest and together will raise their offspring. Other early winter breeders are the red fox, which is monogamous for life, and the beaver, an icon of the northwoods. Included is a list showing some animals and their mating, gestation, and birth times for up north. Valentine's Day can serve as a reminder that there is a plan and purpose for everything in the natural world.

Species	Breeding	Gestation	Birth
Red Fox	Jan/Feb	53 days	Mar/Apr
Beaver	Jan/Feb	120 days	May
Gray Squirrel	Feb	40 days	Mar/Apr
Coyote	Feb	60 days	April
Gray Wolf	Feb	63 days	Apr/May
Gray Fox	Feb/Mar	51 days	Apr/May
Mink	Feb/Mar	51 days	Apr/May
Raccoon	Feb/Mar	64 days	Apr/May
Bobcat	Feb/Mar	62 days	Apr/May

Backyard Buddies

Watching wildlife has become a popular pastime, both indoors and out. Nature shows on television account for over 10% of network programming. In fact, I cannot remember a time when there was not a popular wildlife show on the tube. Perhaps you remember watching *Wild Kingdom* as a child, or currently enjoy episodes of *The Crocodile Hunter* starring the late Steve Irwin. Nature shows are wonderful and bring us up close and personal with wildlife, but unfortunately spoon feed us many weeks worth of footage during a 30 minute show. This creates unreal expectations of nature. We anticipate stepping out in the woods and within minutes seeing eagles, bears, and wolves. Most of us have learned that our wildlife experiences are a matter of being in the right place at the right time, knowing what to look for, and being patient enough (and quiet) to let events unfold before us. But alas, there is hope for the attention span challenged among us. It comes in the form of a fuzzy rodent, with a new episode playing everyday – right out the kitchen window.

Local wildlife watching often falls into three categories. There are the bird watchers, the folks who like to feed the ducks, and the people that can't get enough of the squirrels. Yup, squirrels – love 'em or hate 'em, where there are trees, there are squirrels. They are found in every state and on every continent, with the exception of Antarctica, can occupy a variety of habitats, and eat a wide array of foods. Most squirrels are diurnal (active during the day) and during the winter months have very few predators to contend with. If you live by a woodlot, city park, in the country, or have a bird feeder, you'll see squirrels.

Squirrels belong to the order **Rodentia**. Rodents account for the largest order of mammals and are the most widespread. All are distinguished by their two, large front incisors that grow continually throughout their life. Squirrels are members of the family **Sciuridae**, which is taken from the Latin word *Sciurus*, meaning squirrel. Other members of this family include chipmunks, gophers, woodchucks, and all ground squirrels. The squirrels we often think of, such as the gray squirrel, fox squirrel and red squirrel, also belong to this family, but are considered "tree squirrels."

Tree squirrels live, where else, but in trees. Den holes in large oak trees provide the perfect refuge for most squirrels. Some will make a large nest of leaves and debris in the crotch of a tree. These are called drays and are easy to spot during the winter after the leaves have fallen and exposed the airy abode. Squirrels are active during the day, sometimes during sunup, but more often they venture out several hours after the sun has risen. Mid-day usually finds them back at their den, followed by more activity later in the afternoon, and right up to sundown to complete their day. Days are spend foraging for food, raising their family, and chasing off other squirrels deemed to close for comfort.

Squirrels do not hibernate and will scurry out during inclement weather if food is needed. On extremely cold or inhospitable days squirrels will hunker down and stay in their dens until the weather clears. Like most rodents, populations ebb and flow and are directly linked to seed and nut production from trees, which are also cyclical. Fortunately, we can watch these timber trapeze artists first hand and observe their antics up close. Depending upon where you live, several species may coexist and provide just the distraction to keep you interested and tuned in. More squirrel talk a bit later on…stay tuned!

A Season of Delights

Winter has firmly touched down in the northwoods. Depending on how you look at it, winter is either halfway over, with thoughts turning to spring projects and cures for cabin fever OR winter has only halfway begun, with snowshoe hikes, cross-

15

country ski trips and drives across the lake to Madeline Island, still to come. So far the winter has brought something to please most everyone's palate. In late December, the south shore saw temperatures well into the 40°F range with a few good snow falls. January has seen its share of mild temperatures and the snowfall amounts have been encouraging. The cold arctic air, expected this time of year, has arrived without overstaying its welcome. The nice mix is sure to please outdoor enthusiasts throughout the area.

The winter may seem like a season where plants and animals are frozen in both time and place. While that may be true for our amphibian friends, the reality is that animals destined to stay in the northland year-round have either begun to or are getting ready for their mating season. It may go undetected to some but we know the winter activities provide the spring board for the spring and summer months when "nature" seems abundant.

The winter also welcomes in visitors from the far north. Owls such as the snowy and great gray owl will travel to the southern part of their range to find food. This happens when food supplies drop in the north, when owl numbers increase, and the population cycle of lemmings and hares crash. Look for snowy owls perched atop tall trees or utility poles and hunting over large open fields. Imagine spending your time in the artic tundra of the far north, and your winter break from the extreme cold becomes destination Wisconsin. It's not the Florida Keys, but it sounds delightful to me.

Gray Invasion

As I drove north on WI State Road 35, heading towards Superior, I crossed the county line into Douglas Co. A blanket of fresh snow clung to the conifer trees and the morning sun was just perceptible through the clouds. I spotted one atop a telephone pole. Soon after, another sat perched on a fence post. The one standing watch on the speed limit sign was even bigger. By the time I arrived to the outskirts of Superior, I had counted a total of 14. Yes, the great gray owls had arrived in full force from the great white north.

Much talk has been made about these feathered ghosts from the artic. They have garnered media attention from the Twin Cities, coveted the front page of all the local papers, and stopped traffic along country roads. From Pine County in Minnesota, over into northwestern Wisconsin, and up to Superior, I have seen over 75 gray owls. This past winter would be considered an invasion year for the great grays. The last invasion year was during the winter of 1996-97, and typically run in ten-year cycles, following the population decline of meadow mice, voles, and lemmings.

Great gray owls migrate down from the far northern regions of Canada where the forests meet the tundra. In search of food, they venture south and encounter people and automobiles, which are new to them. Sadly, many grays will not make the return trip north.

They hunt during the day from aspen trees along wooded edges and clearings. With large yellow eyes, a rounded head void of ear tuffs, and grayish-black facial disks, the great gray is a sight to behold. The largest owl has proven there is more to talk about in Wisconsin than the weather.

Winter Survival

For birds that do not migrate to warmer climates during the winter, survival becomes serious business. The challenges are numerous for these small creatures. Birds must deal with the snow that can impede access to food. The cold temperatures increase their loss of body heat and the wind increases the cold and requires more energy output. The winter stress can be overwhelming. So how do the birds survive?

For starters, birds have small bodies (obviously) which produce less body heat than a bigger animal. A small body will also lose heat faster than a bigger body. Thankfully, our hearty winter friends have been created with unique characteristics allowing for winter survival. Many birds will seek shelter in small tree cavities on blustery days, helping to reduce the amount of heat lost (called convection) due to the chilly winds. Birds will put on 50% of extra down and feathers, and while roosting, fluff out their feathers to further reduce heat loss. In addition, flocking together at night helps to conserve heat loss. This is only part of the strategy.

Birds resort to continuous shivering to stay warm. This increases their body heat. If you have a backyard feeder you will notice that it needs constant refilling. Another strategy birds engage in is to simply eat constantly. Continually taking in energy is a way to combat energy lost.

Finally, some birds such as the black-capped chickadee, allow their body temperature to drop during periods of inactivity. The chickadee has a normal body temperature of 109° F. When the ambient air temperature drops below 65° F the birds begin to shiver. When winter hits, it is more efficient to drop the internal core temperature thus making less difference between internal and external temps and losing less body heat.

With 20-25 species of birds staying in the northwoods during the winter, we witness incredible strategies for survival. These revelations help us to build a kinship and appreciation for the birds and challenges they face. Our winter wonderland would not be the same with out 'em.

Three Cheers for Winter

A winter favorite by bird enthusiasts and nature lovers alike is the cardinal. This could be the most easily recognized bird east of the Great Plains. The male cardinal, *Cardinalis cardinalis*, is known for its bright red feathers, regal crest, and stout orange cone-shaped bill, surrounded by a black mask. The non-migrating cardinal has expanded its range into northern Wisconsin and is now a backyard regular along the south shore of Lake Superior.

Early European settlers gave cardinals their name after being reminded of the cardinals of the Catholic Church who wore red robes and matching caps. Cardinals prefer thick cover and often nest in dense thickets of honeysuckle or conifer stands. They can be heard singing their familiar song high atop balsam or spruce trees early on a winter morning. In the bird world, males do all the singing, but with cardinals, both male and female sing the recognized call: *"what cheer, what cheer, what cheer...birdie, birdie, birdie...cue, cue, cue."*

Cardinals are easily attracted to backyard feeders. They eat from the ground or will feed from a platform feeder on a pole, usually avoiding hanging feeders. Cardinals prefer cracked corn and black sunflower seeds. I would consider them skidderish, as they fly off if they notice I am watching them eat. Late in the winter the male cardinal will crack open the shells and feed the seeds to his mate as part of the mating ritual. The two stay together all year long and are considered excellent parents –both feeding and protecting the young.

Once established around your backyard, the cardinals will brighten any day with their "cheerful" song and splash of color. Watching a pair of cardinals together warms the heart for the hopeless romantic in us all. After all, Valentine's Day is just around the corner.

'Tis better to see a bird often,
and know its preference and ways.
Than to see a rare bird once, check your list,
but never to return its gaze.

Winter's Ghost

I can go all winter without seeing one or I can witness them in abundance. The life of northwoods' kings of camouflage could be described as hare today, gone tomorrow. Of course, I am referring to the snowshoe hare. This dashing denizen of the underbrush fills an important niche in the wild.

The snowshoe hare, *Lepus americanus,* gets its name from the oversize feet that propel it up and over the deep snow. A deep snow actually benefits the hare, allowing it to sit atop the snow and browse conifer twigs, bark, needles, and birch, aspen, and cedar buds that it would otherwise be unable to reach. When food is plentiful and predators few, the snowshoe hare population can explode into the thousands per square mile. This scenario is usually followed by a depletion of food and cover, high mortality rates from predators, and a crash in the population.

Population cycles influence both predators and habitat alike. Predators such as the lynx, wolf, bobcat, and weasel depend on the snowshoe hare for a substantial percentage of their diet. Lynx reportedly rely on hares for over 70% of its diet. Fecundity rates in these wildcats drop during down years. However, the vegetation needed by the hares for both food and cover has a chance to rejuvenate during these times.

Snowshoe hares sport their infamous white coat during the winter. Normally brown or gray during the summer months, the short amount of sunlight and cooler temps trigger the fur to turn

21

white. During a winter without snow, hares become easy targets for hawks and owls.

Hares breed in March and April. The males, called bucks, mate with several females, called does. The buck will defend mating territory and jostle with competing bucks for the affection of a female. A doe may give birth to 2-4 little bunnies, which unlike their cottontail cousins, are born fully furred and able to see. Hares have up to four litters per year.

The best way to see a snowshoe hare is to take a hike through a marginal wetland, bordered by underbrush and trees. Snowshoes often remain motionless to avoid detection, but will sprint across the snow if disturbed. A keen eye is needed to track the speedster over the landscape. With leaps of 15 feet, it is easy to lose sight of these galloping ghosts. Good luck on the bunny trail!

Golden Sun Drops

A welcomed guest at my backyard feeder is the American goldfinch. Although the male's winter plumage is not nearly as bright as it is during the summer, it still brings color to the feeder on a cloudy day.

Males lose the distinctive black cap during winter in favor for a dull yellow, while females tend to have a golden hue from the neck down, both with distinctive wing bars. Watch for the characteristic undulating flight pattern as it approaches.

Often dozens of goldfinches will vie for a spot at the tube feeder eating everything that is offered. During the summer, goldfinches are fond of thistle, dandelion, and sunflowers. They will eat thistle seeds and use the soft tops of the seeds for the lining of their nests late into the summer months.

Goldfinches are seen in open countrysides, prairies, weedy fields, and in spruce trees. These "wild canaries" sing an endless song of trills and twitters. Listen for the *per-chic-o-ree* and *zwe-zeeee* call in flight. The sun may be behind the clouds but the goldfinch brings a drop of color to your backyard.

Cold Hard Facts

Temperatures plummeted to -55°F at Couderay, Wisconsin on February 4, 1996.

To calculate windchill, first multiply wind speed x 1.5 and subtract from air temperature. Air temp – (wind speed x 1.5) = windchill.

Beware of the Pogonip!

Pogonip is the term used to describe the rare occurrence of frozen fog. Native Americans used the word to refer to the frozen fog of fine ice needles that form in the mountain valleys in the western United States. According to legend, to breathe the fog was to cause certain death. Thankfully, this has proven to be untrue.

Beak Neck Speed

While sitting and watching my bird feeder, I have noticed different feeding behavior of many birds. There are those that do "fly-bys," simply taking one seed and off to a tree they go. Some perch at the tube feeder and eat for minutes on end. While others land in the middle of the platform and pop one seed after another into their mouth. Have you ever wondered why different birds have different feeding habits? It all has to do with their bills. We'll try and crack open this subject further.

Starting with the "polite" feeders, we have birds such as the black-capped chickadee, red-breasted nuthatch, and white-breasted nuthatch. They will take one seed at a time, typically a black oil sunflower seed, and fly off to a tree branch or shrub. There they hold the shell by their feet, or as with the nuthatches, wedge it into the bark, and repeatedly strike it with their bill. The seed is then swallowed followed by more trips back to the feeder.

Many birds can crack open the shell and extract the seed in their bill. Purple finches, grosbeaks, juncos, redpolls, and cardinals have grooved upper bills and simply crack open the shell, separate the husk, and swallow the seed, all in a matter of seconds. Using a pair of binoculars, watch one of these birds feed and you will see the efficient and messy way they eat.

Many folks lament over blue jays at their feeders. Most of us have seen blue jays land in our feeder and gorge themselves, swallowing seed after seed whole, while depreciating our stock of sunflower seeds. They fill up their gullet with dozens of seeds, then fly off to a safe spot, regurgitate them, crack them open, or stash the seeds away for later. Because of the blue jay's powerful bill, there is no nut to tough for it to crack.

Some birds, such as pigeons, grouse, mourning doves, and turkeys are able to swallow seeds whole. The seeds end up in a part of the stomach called the gizzard, where it is ground up until the seed opens. Most often these birds are ground feeders and do the task of cleaning up around the bird feeder.

Observation of our backyard feeders can bring enjoyment and insight into the world of birds. Watching for subtle behaviors, repeated again and again, make us better observers of the natural world we live in and provide topics (instead of the weather) for us to talk about with our neighbors.

Seed Preference Chart

	Cracked Corn	Peanut	Millet	Safflower	Niger	Black Oil Sunflower	Suet
Black Capped Chickadee		*		*	*	*	*
Blue Jay	*	*				*	*
Cardinal	*	*				*	
Evening Grosbeak	*	*				*	
Goldfinch	*	*	*		*	*	
Indigo Bunting	*	*			*		
Junco	*	*		*	*	*	
Mourning Dove	*		*	*		*	
Pine Siskin		*	*		*	*	
Purple Finch	*	*	*		*	*	
Red Breasted Nuthatch		*		*	*	*	*
Rose Breasted Grosbeak	*			*		*	
Song Sparrow	*				*	*	
Eastern Towhee	*	*				*	
Tufted Titmouse					*	*	
White Breasted Nuthatch	*	*		*	*	*	*
White Throated Sparrow	*			*	*	*	
Woodpeckers	*	*				*	*

Tips for Winter Feeding

Backyard birdfeeders provide extra food for the birds and enjoyment for us while watching them. Some folks have specific goals when it comes to backyard feeders. Attracting the bird species you wish to see is predicated on the food you put out, the shrubs and trees that provide cover, and the type of feeder you assemble.

The Seed Preference Chart is a guide for the types of food that some bird species prefer. During the winter, you may not see as many birds based on your location (northern areas will have fewer) or the severity of the season. Black oil sunflower seeds are generally considered the best food for attracting the largest variety of birds. Putting out different types of seeds will ensure a healthy mix of bird types.

Some birds, such as cardinals, chickadees, and woodpeckers, need the cover of shrubs or trees close by the feeder. The trees can serve as a place to crack open the seeds or provide a safe haven for birds that are less tolerant of disturbances around the feeder. Locate your feeder in a place that is observable, yet next to a sheltered area for the birds.

Lastly, consider hanging several types of feeders. Platform feeders are excellent in providing a place for birds to feed with easy observation. Make sure there is a simple roof over the platform feeder. Hanging covered feeders are also very popular for birds. They provide a good place to eat but can be tossed about by the wind and easily emptied if a squirrel should get into it. Hanging tube feeders, with lots of feeding stations are ideal for finches. Not only do they present great observation opportunities, but the seeds that spill out provide food for the ground feeding birds such as sparrows, juncos, mourning doves, and grouse. Call me if you have specific questions or consult an Audubon Chapter near you.

Muskrat Love

Have you ever wondered what would happen if you put a muskrat in your bathtub? Well, wonder no longer because I have a "tail" to tell. There are times in our lives when we get outside of our comfort zone, and when an opportunity, or so it seems, presents itself, and we simply follow the natural course of events.

It all happened one cold afternoon in February. A muskrat was walking down the street and as fate would have it, our paths crossed. What was a muskrat doing walking down a small town street? I have no idea, although I have heard about strange behaviors of muskrats before, usually in the spring and probably having to do with territorial issues or searching for a mate. Several residents voiced concerns regarding the muskrat presence and without much thought I quickly escorted the furry visitor into a small cage.

The weather was chilly that day and my plans were to relocate the critter to the nearest waterway. Before I was ready to catch and release, I surmised that the muskrat may be hungry, and perhaps, in search of food. So off to the store I went, returning shortly with fresh lettuce. The little fur ball quickly started munching on the greens and spent the rest of the afternoon eating and resting quietly.

As I thought about where to take the mammal, it occurred to me that all the local waterways were frozen. The forecast called for below freezing temps all week with snow likely. Obviously, I could not release it under these circumstances. I decided to bring the muskrat home and keep it as a guest until the weather turned warmer. And that's what I did.

I fixed up the cage with some newspapers, wood block and twigs for chewing, and fresh water. My research revealed that muskrats will eat corn, but need to spend plenty of time in water. The perfect solution – days would be spent in the cage resting and nights spent in the bathtub. That muskrat really seemed to enjoy floating around in the tub. It devoured the corn and lettuce, and for a treat I picked up a few minnows from the local bait shop. Muskrats love little fishies!

The week went by without any problems and the muskrat appeared no worse for wear. By the weekend the weather warmed up and I took my little guest out to the marsh. With little fanfare and a quick adios, off it went into the weeds and out of sight. Now, I'm not one to take in strays, and I generally have a "let nature takes its course" attitude, but I tell you this – I'll never forget the week I had with a muskrat in my bathtub.

Know Your Neighbors?

The nuthatch is a common bird in the northwoods and throughout the midwest. We have two species in Wisconsin: white breasted and red breasted. Both have solid black caps and the red breasted is smaller and has a black eye stripe. White breasted nuthatches are found in mixed forests and reds seem to favor coniferous forests, often seen with black capped chickadees.

If the bird world has nerds, then nuthatches should fall into this category. They can be seen climbing down the trunks of trees head first, searching for insects nestled in the bark. The song, if you can call it that resembles a nasal *"yank, yank, yank."* The red's song is even more nasal and usually faster, but not as loud. These upside down, nasal singing birds are one of my favorites.

They stay in the northwoods year-round are easily attracted to feeders. They love black-oil sunflower seeds! I have a platform feeder and enjoy watching the birds feed. They come in waves, usually taking one seed at a time. The whites feed first, followed by the reds, and then the chickadees. The reds let out a comical, rapid series of "yanks" as they are chased of by other whites and dominate reds, although no bird goes away hungry. Nuthatches generally tolerate close proximity by humans, and these energetic, acrobatic birds are quite enjoyable to watch as they provide year-round company for nature lovers.

The invariable mark of wisdom is to
see the miraculous in the common.
~Ralph Waldo Emerson

Fly By Night

It is a cold and starry night in the northwoods. The distant cry of a coyote and lonesome note from a great horned owl are the only sounds for miles. The stillness seems unbreakable as the trees silhouette the night sky reaching for the moon. With all the bats in hibernation and owls keeping a watchful eye from their perch, the airwaves appear eerily calm. But with the snap of a twig and the bounce of a branch, the forest canopy springs into life. From out of the darkness, riding the wind, comes the original rocketeer rodent – the flying squirrel.

Flying squirrels, both northern and southern species, are abundant mammals which most of us never get to witness. They take to the night shift and glide across the timber highways of the forest. Flying squirrels cannot actually fly, but rather launch themselves into the air. Furred flaps of skin, running the length of their body, provide the aerodynamics needed for jumps of well over 50 feet, as their 6 inch tail serves to keep them on course and out of harm's way.

Flying squirrels are found throughout the upper midwest, Canada, and south to the Gulf of Mexico. They are small rodents, weighing only a quarter of a pound, with tan, reddish or brown fur, and a grayish belly, and have very large eyes. Flying squirrels need a well developed forest in which to live, preferably a mature coniferous or mixed woodland. Their diet consists of mushrooms, nuts, acorns, berries, seeds, and tree lichens. They tend to be more social than their daytime

counterparts, and many will congregate together and share the same tree cavity.

If possible, leave several feeders full of corn or nuts out during the nighttime and watch from a darkened room for these denizens of the dark to come a calling. Do not be surprised when several "drop in" for the free meal. Flying squirrels are certainly unique in their habits as well as in their design, and play an important role in the forest community as they fly by night.

Farewell to Winter

Wrapped inside a thick coat, upon layers of thermal clothing, feet tucked in big comfortable boots, with only two eyes peering out onto the frozen landscape. Venturing out on a day in winter, when the mercury barely tops the single digits, the wind snarling at your back, and the clenching cold air stinging your cheeks, can feel more like a walk on the moon than a hike in the northwoods. Amidst all the inconveniences winter may bring, its allure, fascination, and unveiling mysteries provide the tonic I need to slow down and connect with the natural history of the place I call home.

Emotions run high during the season of winter. The giddiness of the first snowfall, followed by the rush of the holiday season, and the drain of short days, arctic cold fronts and the stress of travel, can become a rollercoaster event, leaving us tired and irritable. Thankfully, the season that may bring out the Mr. Hyde in all of us, can also provide a Dr. Jekyll cure. The elixir is found in its simplicity.

31

There is something so simple, so therapeutic, and so bombastically benign about walking in the winter. Perhaps it is the "swish" of snow under my feet - feeling as if I am walking through granulated sugar. The snow then compresses and deflates, and becomes the crunch of peanut shells on a hardwood floor. Walking across a drift and riding the top of the crust will test my balance and faith. Witnessing the undulations across a frozen wetland will spur my imagination. And listening to the silence after a snowfall will bring me closer to the truth.

The truth is that I am on this planet for a short time. I can spend my time chasing down deadlines and filling my life with clutter, or I can go out and enjoy my surroundings, learning the lessons of nature. Surroundings that need basic observations, require simple yet profound explanations, and fill a role and play a part that yields to a greater purpose. The natural history of the land serves as a touchstone from which I can live my life with peace and comfort. If I can "see" the connections in nature, then perhaps I will be able to "see" my place on earth more clearly.

After a healthy snowfall, I enjoy heading out and watching the rebirth of the landscape. The trees come to life during this time. Balsam firs and red pines are flocked with snow, which will shed their loads with the slightest breeze. As the limbs let go, the snow hisses as it falls, and the branches spring back up, as if giving a gentle wave in my direction. A few birds, usually blue jays and chickadees, emerge to forage and their calls are hushed by the blanket of white. Chickadees, always curious, often flit by at my presence and offer a song to lift my soul. Periods of noticeable stillness overtake me and soak my mind with a unique calmness known only to the forest in winter.

Before I complete my journey I follow the tracks of deer, cottontails, gray squirrels, and fisher. Each set tells a story and fuels my sense of wonder and amazement at the tenacity of life sustained here in the woods. With so much to see, and unexplored rivers, bogs, and forests to discover, the winter always goes by too fast. Snow drifts decay, the winds shift, and the sun climbs higher in the sky, amounting to winter's passage. It is truly a special season. One that can capture the spirit, unlock nature's mystery, and actually warm the soul. Until next year, I bid winter a fond farewell and carry its message into the coming spring.

Aye, starry-eyed did I rejoice
With marvel of a child,
And there were those who heard my voice
Although my words were wild:
So as I go my wistful way,
With worship let me sing,
And treasure to my farewell day
God's Gift of Wondering.

- Robert Service

SPRING

Little Dipper

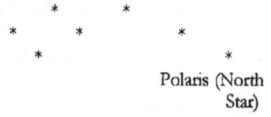

Polaris (North Star)

Big Dipper

Trillium

One attraction in coming to the woods to
live was that I should have leisure
and opportunity to see the Spring come in.
~Henry David Thoreau

Rise and Shine

Climbing ever so higher in the sky, you can feel the warmth of the sun on your face. We are entering into the season of beginnings and renewal. The word spring comes from the ancient Anglo-Saxon word for "rising," German *springan* meaning "to jump" and Old English, as an act of leaping. Whichever the word source for the season, it is clear that activity is at hand. Our response to spring is to venture out and experience first hand the wonder and beauty in nature that surrounds us. The challenge is this: find a quiet spot outside, free from traffic noise and the like, sit still for fifteen minutes and simply listen and observe. Your senses will thank you!

Spring is officially welcomed on March 20th this year, and ushers in the plans and preparations from the winter's exiles and excursions. The spring equinox contains an equal length of day and night, after which the amount of daylight gains several minutes every day leading up to summer. The sun rises from due east on March 20th and sets due west. Set your sun dials accordingly and get out to great our morning star.

If you doubt that spring has arrived and the evidence of 20°F days, snow on the ground, and your Bermuda shorts still at the

35

bottom of the dresser drawer, proves your disbelief, take heart —I've got good news to tell. Signs of spring abound! Here are a few I have noticed: Snow geese spotted heading north on their way to Canada and beyond. Looking down on the snow, little peppers of movement from springtails, commonly called snow fleas. Springtails are insects that eat decaying plant matter and "flip" inches above the snow. Chickadees are singing their mating song, *"fee be, fee be be."* Eagles are very active. Sightings include their aerial courtship displays and nest building and repairing. South facing slopes are snow-free revealing old leaves and grass. And lastly, the potholes on the road have opened up, inviting us and our vehicles to go for a swim. Personal floatation devices encouraged!

Springtime Serenade

Most everyone looks for that first robin to signal the official start of spring. That is, everyone but me. No, I prefer to walk down to the local marsh and listen for the sound of spring and the call of the red-winged black bird.

Red-winged black birds are often the first migratory birds to arrive up north. The males show up in mid-March while marshes are still frozen. They'll eat seeds, cattails, and look for hibernating caterpillars. The male red-wings stake out territory in the marsh and defend the area in hopes of attracting a female.

Male red-winged black birds are medium-sized songbirds, with jet-black feathers and scarlet epaulets (shoulder patches) with a yellow line beneath. Females look like large brown, heavily streaked sparrows, which camouflage well in their marsh nests. Males sing the loud and familiar *"conk-cor-ree"* to attract a mate and defend their territory. Another common call is the "high whistle" usually sung in nearby treetops.

Nests are small grass baskets, constructed on cattails, three to seven feet above the ground. Red-wing eggs are the size of a grape, usually 3-5 in a nest, and are black/purple speckled or streaked light blue-green. Incubation lasts 10 days and chicks become fledglings in two weeks.

By September, both young and old will gear up for migration — heading south to Texas and Florida. The red-winged black bird is common throughout the mid-west, found in every state, and believed to be the most numerous single species of land bird in North America, with fall populations estimated at 190 million. With so many birds, I am assured to hear *"conk-cor-ree"* and have a head start on spring.

Wings of Spring

It is not uncommon to have snow on the ground during the first week of April. However, do not let a little snow keep you off the trails, for you may be rewarded for your efforts. Mourning cloak butterflies are typically out and about by April, adding grace and beauty to the spring landscape.

The mourning cloak, *Nympphalis antiopa*, emerges from winter hibernation in search of food and a mate. It has toughed out the winter (as an adult) under the protection of logs, woodpiles, and loose bark. By late March, these winged wonders flutter along forest edges and openings, and along meadows, streams, roadsides, and parks. The mourning cloak has dark brown to maroon colored wings, with a cream yellow border and blue spots just inside the border. The butterfly's common name comes from its resemblance to the dark coats worn by mourners grieving the loss of a loved one.

Mourning cloaks belong to the family of brushfoots – meaning they have shortened forelegs covered with long hairs. Often, with the earliest butterfly of the year, comes the question of what does it eat? Since no flowers are in bloom the mourning cloak searches out sap oozing from trees with broken branches or sapsucker holes. They also eat rotting fruit fallen from orchard trees.

After mourning cloaks mate, the female lays her fertilized eggs on willow or aspen leaves. Soon after, the mourning cloak dies and the next generation of caterpillar reappears in late summer. These new mourning cloaks will live into the fall and hibernate throughout the winter. These "wings of spring" must truly have the spirit of the northwoods.

Test of Time

When hiking through the woods, you may see many trees that have their tops damaged or missing, or simply have no foliage on them at all. These are called snags and are caused by lightning strikes, windthrow, disease or decay. Snags play an important role in the environment providing dens, nests, feeding sites, food storage, perching, preening, and courtship ritual sites to a large variety of wildlife.

There are two types of standing snags – hard snags and soft snags. Hard snags have rotted out centers with a solid exterior. These make great den trees. Soft snags maintain their soft pulpy wood fiber making perfect feeding sites for insect eating birds.

Once the snag falls, it can also provide a home for salamanders, frogs, snakes, small mammals, and rodents. The decaying tree will put nutrients back into the forest floor and provide a rich habitat for new plants or a tree to grow from. If this happens it is called a "nurse log."

Whether standing or fallen, snags play an important role in the forest. They provide homes for many creatures that require cavities to live in. Often the cavities are made by woodpeckers searching for insects such as termites and carpenter ants in the trunk. Songbirds, owls, mammals, and rodents will all use snags for a home. Look for these critter condos on your next hike. The tree may have fallen but it is not easily forgotten.

Men are like trees; each one must put forth the leaf that is created in him."

~Henry W. Beecher

A Symphony of Spring

My favorite part of spring is when I hear the frogs start calling. Once emerged from their winter slumber, male frogs begin to sing – staking out territory and attempting to attract a mate. It is one of the many auditory pleasures of spring. For many, frogs represent a first hands-on experience with nature. Collecting tadpoles and catching frogs seem to be universal pastimes for youth. Frogs play an important role in our world, by not only providing sensory pleasure, but also as indicator species reflecting the condition of the local environment.

Frogs are amphibians, which means "both life forms" and refers to their life in both water and on land. Frogs start out as eggs in water and then hatch into tadpoles. There they feed on aquatic plants such as algae and use internal gills to obtain oxygen. After metamorphosis has taken place, (the changing from tadpole to adult frog) frogs will move onto land, breath with lungs and through their skin, and become carnivorous, eating flies, moths, beetles, and ants. Their semi-permeable skin makes them sensitive to toxins in the environment, thus becoming indicator species.

Frogs spend time in damp cool places during the day. They are cold-blooded and need moist habitats to prevent from drying out. Frogs are most active during the night and are found near shallow ponds, wetlands, and closed canopy forests. Breeding behavior for frogs usually begin within three periods corresponding to water temperatures. These are early spring, late spring, and summer. I listed the frogs we can expect to hear, with brief physical characteristics and a description of their call.

Wood Frog: Usually one of the first frogs to start singing near shallow pools of water. Look for them in forested areas. A very small, brownish frog with a dark mask through its eyes. Call is like a clucking or quacking.

Chorus Frog: Another early spring caller, the chorus frog likes marshes, wet prairies, and wetlands. It has brown stripes running down its back, with a stripe through its eye. The call is like running your thumb across the teeth of a plastic comb.

Spring Peeper: The spring peeper has an "X" on its back and is light tan in color. They are found in forest areas and woodlots, and breed in wet areas close by. Call is a very high "peep" and many together produce a high trill sounding like sleigh bells.

Gray Tree Frog: Their color can change from gray to green and will blend in exceptionally well with their background. They have very noticeable toe pads and are found in wooded areas usually resting on the trunks of trees. Call is a short, raspy, bird-like trill.

Northern Leopard Frog: This frog has green or light brown skin and large round dark spots all over its body. They only live about two years and use a variety of wetlands. The call is like a loud broken snore.

Green Frog: The green frog is dark olive with small brown spots. Found in permanent waters like deep marshes, large ponds, and lakes. Call is like a loose banjo string being plucked.

Bull Frog: The bullfrog is light to dark green and the biggest of Wisconsin's frogs. Require permanent water because the tadpoles do not metamorphose until the second year. Call is a deep "jug-o-rum" or low "fried rice."

Our backyards and wooded areas come alive with music each spring. Frog calls are perfect for falling asleep to and add to any camping atmosphere. On your next twilight stroll, stop by the local wetlands and hear who is calling or visit the local environmental agency to see if you can participate in frog surveys. Enjoy the symphony of spring!

Crafty by Nature

Easily recognized by the conspicuous black eye mask and ringed tail, the raccoon has become one of the most notorious mammals throughout the country. The success of the raccoon population lies in their ability to live in a variety of habitats and survive on a flexible diet. The raccoon's Latin name is *Procyon lotor*. Lotor means "one who washes." It is suggested that captive raccoons will sometimes dip their food into water before eating it.

The raccoon is found throughout the United States, except in areas of the Rocky Mountains. Forests and wooded areas are preferred, with old hardwood trees for nesting sites and a close proximity to water. The raccoon is a solitary mammal and will feed along waterways eating fish, crayfish, frogs, turtle eggs, and insects. They will also eat young birds, bird eggs, nuts, fruits, and grains, particularly corn.

Mating begins in February or March, with three to six kits being born approximately 63 days later. Dens are usually in hollow trees. The young coons stay with the mother until they are a year old. It is common to encounter a mother with her young in the forest during late summer. I have run into several families along the North Country Trail in Ashland County. They are nocturnal and will often appear right after dusk.

Raccoons are hunted for their fur and can also be eaten, reportedly tasting like turkey or lamb. Raccoons are often viewed as pests because of their propensity to adapt to human presence and opportunistic ways of getting food. Town dumps, garages, cabins, and campsites are common destinations for these clever creatures. The curious and crafty nature of raccoons set them apart as one of nature's most legendary animals.

Where Eagles Dare

The story of the bald eagle in North America could easily be turned into a big screen movie. This classic riches to rags to riches drama has all the trappings of a Hollywood blockbuster, and the best part is we do not have to waste our $8.50 to see it – it is waiting right outside our back door.

The bald eagle became our nation's symbol in 1782 and has been a source of pride ever since. One eagle even went into battle during the Civil War with a Wisconsin regiment. Local schoolchildren (including myself *many* years ago) learn about the honored eagle "Old Abe" when visiting the state capital building in Madison. Fast-forward almost 200 years and the bald eagle is fading fast from the American landscape.

In the mid-seventies, the status of the eagle had taken a turn for the worst. Urban sprawl, unrestricted use of pesticides such as DDT, illegal hunting, and lakeshore development, combined to put the eagle on the endangered species list. Conservationists alike and books such as Rachel Carson's *Silent Spring* exposed the public to the plight of the bald eagle. Efforts were made and laws were evoked to aid in the recovery efforts of this inspiring raptor.

Today, thankfully, through conservation and education, the bald eagle can be commonly seen throughout Wisconsin. Large white pine trees that grace the lakeshores of the northwoods are often home to mating pairs of eagles. White pines can withstand the weight of the massive nests, often weighing over a ton, that are built upon year after year as the monogamous pair return to raise their brood.

The juvenile eagles remain dark brown and their heads and tails do not turn white until the fourth year. Bald eagles require open water for catching fish, and supplement their diet with rodents, snakes, or commonly scavenge off road kill. I frequently see bald eagles perched on the carcasses of deer along the highways.

I always stop to take in a bald eagle sighting. The sheer size and magnitude of the bird is overwhelming, but also the recovery efforts made by folks that did not want to let this creature become just another part of history, is heart felt. As with any national symbol, the eagle means so much to so many people. If the story were ever to become a movie, I might have to rethink my finances and go see it, and maybe get popcorn too!

Sweet Spring Singer

No doubt you have heard it countless times. It comes from the alder thicket, the hedgerow, and the wetlands. From the Pacific Northwest to the Atlantic Coast, with subtle variances in color and call, the song sparrow's reputation as a melodious singer is only surpassed by the longevity of its song.

The song sparrow, *Melospiza melodia,* is an ubiquitous, well known sparrow that arrives to the northwoods in late March and early April. I have often taken walks along willow and alder thickets in March, while the ground is still covered in snow, and heard this siren of spring. I have to look carefully to find the vocalist since their streaked brown back and streaked white breast blend in so well with the surroundings. The most pronounced clue for identification is the large dark spot located centrally on the breast. But it is the song sparrow's recital that endears it to bird lovers everywhere.

As the male song sparrow begins to sing, he throws his head upward and lets forth a long melody. In the classic text, *Birds of America,* one author states, "He seems intent upon sending his little prayer of thankfulness straight up to heaven, by the shortest route." The call actually starts with a series of single notes, usually three, followed by a complex string of trills, twitters, buzzes and whistles. Some ornithologists have put it to the rhythm of *"maids, maids, maids, put on your tea kettle, ettle, ettle."*

Both male and female song sparrows stay busy all summer raising two broods, which when fledged will return the following

45

spring to continue the concert recitals. Eating weed seeds, berries, beetles, ants, and wasps, the song sparrow does its part in nature's delicate balance. With nicknames such as ground sparrow, hedge sparrow, silver tongue, and swamp finch, it is easy to see that this sparrow gets around and spreads its sweet song of spring everywhere it goes.

Winds of Change

There comes a day when we know spring has arrived. Rather than relying on the calendar for proof, it happens while we are out in the yard or walking through the local park. Noticeably, the winds are out of the south and the smell of soil and grasses fill the air. This awareness opens the gates of spring riding on the winds of change.

And what is wind? Is it the tangible sound of wind driven rain and rustling leaves, or watching dust devils twirl and trees swaying with the breeze? Perhaps it is the feeling of having no beginning and no end, a harbinger of change, or the "just out of reach" quality of Solomon's "chasing after the wind" and Dylan's "blowing in the wind."

Scientists have recognized wind as a product of two pressure gradients. Wind occurs when air rushes from a high-pressure zone to a low-pressure zone. The greater the difference in pressure, the stronger the wind. Wind evaporates moisture on the skin and removes heat energy - called convection. This is why a breeze in the late spring cools us on a warm day.

Francis Beaufort, a British Admiral, invented a wind scale in 1805. The Beaufort Scale is still the standard of wind measurement used by mariners, pilots, and forest rangers. Take a look outside and see the influence of wind: as an agent of erosion, disperser of seeds and pollen, and as an usher of weather patterns. Before I take to the wind, I'll conclude with an old proverb, "a backing wind means storms are nigh; a veering wind will clear the sky."

Predaceous Pals

Of all the insects that could accompany you on your walk through the woods, I wonder how many would be welcomed companions? I admit that even I avoid certain trails during times of the year because of the multiplicity of mosquitoes, deer flies, and ticks. However, if I could invite the services of just one insect – it would assuredly be the green darner dragonfly.

Dragonflies are the most fearsome fliers of the northwoods. Thankfully their diet is confined to insects and not humans. In fact, dragonflies can be quite protective during a hike. I have benefited often from their presence, witnessing as they snatch deer flies from in front of my head. As great escorts, dragonflies will patrol and defend their territory while gleaning the sky of bothersome insects.

The green darner dragonfly appears in mid-April. Interestingly, some populations of green darners overwinter in the larvae stage and emerge from the icy waters as nymphs. Some are migratory and fly north in the springtime. Green darners are typically the largest, fastest, and most common species in the northwoods. All dragonflies hold their wings horizontal, or down, during rest. Green darners have a green thorax (the middle part of the body from which the wings are attached to) and a long, bright blue abdomen or "tail."

Two noticeable features of the green darner are the wings and eyes. The wingspan is over four inches wide and enable the green darner to fly at speeds of 35 mph. Dragonflies make acrobatic maneuvers in flight and can stop on a dime, fly backwards, and catch mosquitoes, horse flies, black flies, butterflies, and other dragonflies. The eyes are a large, bulging, compound feature, which provide a 360° field of vision. Eighty percent of the dragonfly's brain capacity is devoted to eyesight.

Green darners stay in flight until mid-October. Typically, adults mate in mid-air, after which the female deposits her eggs in slow moving waters such as marshes and ponds. The eggs develop into nymphs that grow under water and are just as fierce as the adults. When nymphs are ready to transform into adults, they climb out of the water onto a reed or cattail stem and emerge from their exoskeleton to dry off and pump life into their wings. Watch for and collect a few of the exoskeletons on your next canoe trip as you travel along shorelines and sloughs.

Green darners can live up to ten weeks. They generally spend morning hours basking in the sun before they set off on their midday hunts. These marauding mosquito hawks are great to watch, study, and identify, and have the ability to turn us all into bug lovers. Happy hiking!

On The Wet Trail …

As the snow melts and spring rains fall, the lowlands in the forests become breeding grounds of life. Often shallow and depressed, ephemeral wetlands are critical habitats for amphibians and aquatic invertebrates.

In early spring, amphibians such as the wood frog and spotted salamander migrate from upland wooded areas, down to these vernal pools to breed. The aqueous environment provides a safe place to lay eggs and develop without predation from fish. In the case of the wood frog, the tiny tadpoles will grow, eat aquatic vegetation, then emerge as frogs before the wetland dries up, and spend the remainder of the summer in the forest.

A variety of plants and wildlife benefit from ephemeral wetlands. Species such as Blanding's turtle, spring peeper, blue flag iris, little green heron, fairy shrimp, and a variety of snails, all use the spring pools. Make a visit to one this season and bask in the oasis of life, and protect these crucial habitats from over development and urban sprawl.

Effulgent Ephemerals

Spring wildflowers hold a special place in my heart. Before the trees can send forth new leaves, and before the fallen ones have turned to mulch, spring wildflowers have a brief window of opportunity to emerge from the soil, bloom in the sun's rays, and jettison its seed for the following year. All while the threat of twelve inches of wet

snow looms in the forecast. So, if a spring flower blooms in the forest and no one is there to see it, is it just as lovely?

One of the earliest and colorful flowers to bloom is hepatica. Hepatica comes in two varieties: round-lobed and sharp-lobed. Found in dry, mixed forests during April, hepatica is a dainty flower that ranges from white, pink, blue, or lavender in color. It has a larger leaf, either round-lobed or sharp-lobed, at the base, from which a hairy stem rises. The flower has 5-9 petal like sepals and 3 green bracts (little leaves) underneath.

Hepatica takes its name from the Latin word meaning "liver." Early botanists saw a resemblance of the round-lobed basal leaf to the liver. Because of this, herbalists often used hepatica to treat liver ailments, but there is no proof that these were effective. Although short is their time to shine, hepatica and all spring wildflowers carry their splendor and grace throughout the northwoods – regardless if anyone is there to see it.

Mini-Croakers

On a brisk spring morning, I was walking a trail along the Flag River in northern Bayfield County. Off in the distance, I heard what sounded like ducks quacking and as I approached closer, the sounds grew louder and then, in an instant – they stopped! This scene brought a smile to my face because it means my favorite amphibian is back, the wood frog.

Wood frogs, *Rana sylvatica*, are usually the first frogs to emerge from winter hibernation. In late March and early April, these frogs awake and head towards the local watering hole for mating. Wood frogs use vernal pools and ephemeral ponds – basically shallow areas of water produced by melting snow and spring rains, which will be dry by the summer. Once there, wood frogs begin singing to attract females. Their call is a series of cluck like croaks, which soon turn into a frantic chorus of quacking.

The mating season lasts only 6-14 days. The female lays over 1,000 eggs in a gelatinous mass on the water, often attached to a twig. The eggs hatch in a week to a month depending on the temperature. Tadpoles finish the metamorphosis by late May. Adult wood frogs spend the rest of their lives in the humid microclimate of a well developed understory under the cool shadows of a closed canopy forest.

Wood frogs are tiny little hoppers, about 1-2 inches long. They are brown with a dark brown "mask" running along the sides of their face, through the eye and back to their shoulder. The days are spent eating beetles, crickets, caterpillars, spiders, and earthworms, while trying to avoid predators such as garter snakes, herons, raccoons, and larger frogs. When the weather turns cold again the wood frogs will sink into the mud and sleep away the winter, surviving subfreezing temperatures thanks to large amounts of glucose pumped through their bodies. This natural antifreeze protects the fragile cells from freezing and becoming damaged.

If you are near a wooded area, chances are good you'll hear this call of the wild. Listen for these mini-croakers on your next walk. Small they are, but a big delight to the senses.

Nature's Song

Everyday it calls without the hype of mass media. No sales pitch needed. I do not need to sell anyone on nature, for nature sells itself. It is the soft sell to be sure of, but a successful transaction none-the-less. This is what I like about nature. Not a lot of whistles and bells, rather subtle statements that play to one's senses, intellect, and emotions. If you ask gardeners, hikers, hunters, anglers, birders, or skiers, what they enjoy most about their hobby or sport, many will simply respond by saying, "I just like getting outside." The freedom of open spaces, scenic vistas framed by large trees, and the gentle sounds of song birds, crickets, and cool breezes, seem to be universally enjoyed by all.

We, the nature lovers, often try to coerce our family and friends to come with us on a canoe trip or take that 9 mile hike, with promises of rare bird sightings, wildlife at our fingertips, and fields of fancy. We really just want to take our passion for nature and make it theirs. The fear is that folks, so used to watching television, with 7-minute intervals, internet, emailing, and cell phone influenced days, will not be held captive by the sweet elixir of nature's song. If I invite my neighbor to go for a hike in the woods that is more sitting and listening, more watching and waiting, and more silence than conversation, I suspect the reaction would be luke warm at best.

So where does it start? I imagine each one of us could tell a story about our first few experiences in nature. In retrospect, most of us did not know "it" was happening at the time, but the connection was made. A mood, feeling, or emotion was established, and consciously or not we sought to repeat those experiences. I do not think we grow out of these connections. Just as many birds return to the same nesting site and fish return to spawning grounds, we too sojourn back to familiar places in nature. So take time today and remember, rekindle, and enjoy nature's song.

> One has to be alone, under the sky, before everything falls into place and one finds their own place in the midst of it all.
>
> ~Thomas Merton

Around the Bend

Spring weather is certainly unpredictable, but fortunately, sightings and occurrences are more calendar friendly. As I check my phenology records I can expect to see juncos by the first of April, flickers a week later, and trilliums in bloom by the end of April. Having local records from previous years is a nice way to know what to look for during my hikes and another way to stay in touch with my surroundings.

Male goldfinches are molting and will soon be sporting their bright yellow plumage. Watch for garter snakes to emerge from hibernation and soak up some vitamin D. Yellow warblers and ovenbirds will be up north by May, and watch out for turtles, as they seem to fall victim to many automobile tires. Better yet, lend a helping hand as they cross the road, returning to their nesting grounds.

Finally, if you've never participating in tapping trees, this is the year to do it. Find a local club or nature center and volunteer with them, or tap several maple trees in your backyard. The experience is priceless and you'll really appreciate the sweet auburn nectar in a whole new way.

Pileated Woodchipper

The woods come alive with this loud and lively bird. The pileated woodpecker is the largest woodpecker in North America, and although found throughout Canada and the eastern United States, I like to think of this as a "northwoods" bird. Imagine walking through a dense mature forest and from the distance you hear a loud *wucka, wucka, wucka,* then a large bird of black and white flashes overhead. When I first heard the pileated's call, it reminded me of howler monkeys in the tropics – something piercing and definitive.

The pileated woodpecker is the size of a large crow with a distinctive red crest. The bill is massive and it has a white chin and white stripe down the sides of the neck. In flight, large white wing patches are visible from underneath its wings. The pileated woodpecker can also be recognized by its loud drumming that will reverberate throughout the woods. Left behind are large rectangular holes in trees, as the pileated searches for ants, wood-boring beetles, berries, and nuts. These cavities make great homes for other birds, rodents, and bats. A large pile of wood chips and debris are also evidence of the woodpecker's presence.

These birds were once known as "logcocks" and more recently have become known as the "Woody Woodpecker" bird. The pileated seems to be shy and does not tolerate close proximity by humans, although I had the distinct pleasure of watching two engage in a courtship on an aspen tree branch while I peered out through a window into my backyard. Keep your ears open for this giant signature of the north and you may get a glimpse of one of nature's most creative creations.

The Common Pilgrim

A dubious crime has been perpetrated on the American public. A crime so hideous that, as a naturalist, I must combat it on a daily basis and with great force. The crime of which I am speaking is the relegation of the common and simple to the level of overlooked and insignificant. In nature, this cannot be tolerated. To further my case, with evidence soon at hand, I present exhibit a: Canada mayflower.

A delightful spring flower, Canada mayflower is found throughout the upper third of the country, from Maine to Montana, well into Canada, and even as far south as Georgia. As a member of the lily family, this common plant goes by many names, including wild lily of the valley, *Maianthemum canadense*, may lily, bead ruby, chipmunk berry, and the ever-so-unflattering "false lily of the valley."

By late April, these spring pilgrims send tightly curled leaves up through the leaf litter and produce a glossy green carpet on the forest floor. Underground stems connecting the flowers sprout new shoots that are genetically identical. In late May some plants will bloom, (many never do) producing a small white cluster of star-shaped petals and a sweet fragrance. The entire plant is usually only six inches tall.

A month after blooming, little green berries form that will later turn dull red. The berries are consumed by chipmunks, mice, hares, and grouse. Canada mayflower will remain above ground until the beginning of autumn. Perhaps because of its size, or perhaps due to its ubiquitous nature in both geography and habitat, the wild lily of the valley is often mistakenly overlooked and underappreciated in the spring flora. Let's not be guilty of passing up this common flower as insignificant, but rather bask in its fortitude and modest beauty.

Flights of Fancy

Spring migration is under way and an early returnee to the northwoods is the tree swallow. In a race to find the prime nesting sites, tree swallows are the first of all the swallows to venture north and lay claim to their territory. In addition to arriving on the heels of spring, they also carry a message of hope.

Tree swallows represent blessings and fertility in cultures from Greece to China. Bad luck would come from killing the bird or destroying its nest. The name swallow comes from a Scandinavian name *svalow*, meaning to console. This originates from the belief that swallows comforted Jesus at his crucifixion. Many are familiar with and celebrate the return of swallows to San Juan Capistrano, in Southern California each year at the end of March.

Tree swallows set up shop in late April and May, using tree cavities for nesting sites. They will readily use human-made boxes, but need to compete with bluebirds and house sparrows for the space. They prefer nesting sites near water, such as beaver ponds or wetlands, and will also nest along prairies or meadows that are adjacent to a lake.

True acrobats of the air, it seems that tree swallows spend more time in flight than they do at rest. They can fly up to 20 miles per hour and glide in circles as they hunt for insects to eat. There can be up to six hatchlings in the nest and it is estimated the chicks are fed every three minutes. The adult swallows stay busy for three weeks until the young chicks become fledglings.

Their bluish-green back and white underside give the tree swallow a streamlined appearance, as they are entertaining to watch. Remarkably, tree swallows can be one of the last birds to leave the northwoods and head south to Florida and the Gulf of Mexico. Often they will migrate in large number and form huge flocks upon their arrival south. It is remarkable how much reverence and history can come with such a simple bird. Hopefully that trend will continue for the next generation – for both us and them.

Keep On Keepin' On

Most folks know they can expect to see their first robin in mid-to-late March. Another widely held "truth" is that corn should be "knee-high by the 4th of July." Common sayings and beliefs are based on experience and observation. Looking at the relationships between climate, seasonal changes, and naturally occurring events is called phenology. We know from experience and research that changes in nature, such as birds migrating and flowers blooming, usually follow a progression as the season grows. Before sharing some springtime phenology, here are a few more old colloquialisms: plant corn when oak leaves become the size of a mouse's ear, and when leaves appear on the lilac - peas, beets, and lettuce should be planted.

Having the opportunity to observe nature's gifts of spring is fun, rewarding, and I consider it a privilege. It also helps to share observations with friends and gather information about what other folks are seeing, especially in your area. There are books and even calendars with weekly information about what you can expect to see. These have helped me to become a better observer of nature. The busy events in April continue on into May and June.

Starting with birds, I spent one evening, right at dusk, listening and watching male woodcocks engage in their courtship display. Ruffed grouse continue to "drum" in fields and woods, northern flickers have taken up residency in backyards and along side of roads (look for the flash of their white rump feathers as they fly off), sandhill cranes feed along wetlands, chipping sparrows are trilling, mother geese are leading recently hatched goslings for walks, and my backyard feeder has greeted goldfinches, purple finches, and been emptied out by grackles, red-winged blackbirds, brown-headed cowbirds, and gray squirrels. The warbler migration has started with yellow-rumped, palm, chestnut-sided, and yellow warblers making their way north. I just saw my first rose-breasted grosbeak in early May, and the waterways are hosting spotted and solitary sandpipers, blue-winged teals, coots, mallards, ringed-necks, mergansers, wood ducks, and loons.

The woods are calling with chorus frogs, spring peepers, leopard frogs, and gray tree frogs, while the grassy areas are humming with common green darner dragonflies, tortoise shells, cabbage whites, gray commas, spring azures, and duskywing butterflies. I've seen both garter and green snakes along the trails, big brown bats at night, mayflies hitchhiking on my arm, mosquitoes probing for a meal, and deer ticks hiding on my pants.

Spring flowers are in bloom and include marsh marigolds, wood anemone, bloodroot, wood violets, skunk cabbage (with enormous leaves), round-lobed hepatica, and trillium just to name a few. Most trees have leafed out with quaking aspen full blown. These are just a few of the things I have seen. Your observations will surely include many of the same items and most likely ones that I did not include.

Continue to look for these signs of spring, along with upcoming events such as, columbine in bloom, morel mushrooms popping up, green frogs and bullfrogs calling, monarch butterflies arriving, black-eyed Susan's, milkweed, and yarrow in bloom, painted turtles laying eggs, and fireflies lighting up the night. The question is where will you be when they happen? I know where I'll be.

A Matter of Taste

Every once in a while I find myself ready to try something completely new, novel, and different. I find it is not only good for my spirit, but it also helps me to see things in a new light. And I have been trying to illuminate my taste buds with edibles from the forest for some time now. My latest adventure – skunk cabbage.

Right away, the name and reputation should send up a red flag, but to see skunk cabbage in the woods, so lush, so green, so tempting, is to understand my situation. (The plant is well known for giving off an odiferous scent of skunk.) Early in the spring I was seeing this woodland plant everywhere I turned. Wherever there was a seep, a small creek, or wet soil, I saw skunk cabbage. The plant can start in late winter, pushing up through the snow with its purplish brown or green-mottled shell like spathe. Inside the spathe is the flower and after it blooms, it puts forth large succulent green leaves. The leaves are up to two feet long and a foot wide, looking like fresh romaine lettuce. I could not imagine something so prominent and tangible would not be in some way edible – and I was right.

I researched the matter and found several uses for skunk cabbage. One source reported that the thoroughly dried leaves are quite good reconstituted in soups. It also said dried rootstocks can be made into a flour. Another source recommended gathering young leaves with their white leaf stocks and boiling the rootstocks until tender and serving with butter and parmesan cheese. One word of caution – the water must be changed several times to rid the acidic quality of the plant.

Skunk cabbage contains calcium oxalate crystals, and if eaten raw causes an intense burning sensation in the mouth. For reasons of personal research and credibility, I sampled the plant raw and agreed 100% with this assessment! There was however, some debate if boiling does in fact remove this property. My sources disagreed on this matter. So, there was only one way to find out.

I collected a handful of fresh leaf stocks and set forth to boil them. I rinsed the stocks before hand, and then started to cook. I changed the water three times, then rinsed, and served with butter, salt and pepper, and a dash of parmesan cheese. After three big bites, I found the texture pleasing, the aroma pleasant, and my mouth was *ON FIRE*! I guess one of my sources was right.

Regardless of the results, I enjoyed the experiment, and will try it again soon. Next time, before I do the cooking, I plan to thoroughly dry the rootstocks. There are plenty of other wild edibles to sample from the forest without concern. Wild strawberries will be ripe soon and teas are always enjoyable - especially white cedar, balsam, and labrador teas. Morel mushrooms are popping up and may I suggest substituting honey instead of sugar for your next baking project. Use honey in place of sugar and add a half-teaspoon of baking soda for every cup used. Using resources straight from nature connects us to the land

and we tend to appreciate the gifts of the season a little more. Good cooking!

Moondance

As dusk settles in, soon giving way to the night, quietness hangs over the forest trail. The grass clearings and fields nearby will soon awaken with a jubilant courtship display. This is no ordinary nightclub scene, but rather the mesmerizing call of nature that comes in the form of the American woodcock.

You've probably heard it all of your life. The short, nasal call, from just over yonder, that comes not long after sundown. Perhaps not the most romantic of calls, but the repeated cry of "*peent*" serves notice that the woodcock is searching for a mate. Their courtship display is certainly unique and fascinating to watch, and requires simply patience and a good set of eyes to witness the festivities.

In the evening the American woodcock flies into a clearing and starts to strut about in the grass. As he does, the call of "*peent*" will be repeated over and over. Then, without warning, the woodcock will take to the sky, flying up in a whirlwind, while creating a whistling and kissing sound. Here's where a good set of eyes is needed. The bird continues this circular flight pattern, then abruptly touches down not far from where it started. The entire process is then repeated, often for hours on end, in hopes of attracting a female. Once on Stockton Island, in Lake Superior, I witnessed dozens of woodcocks flying onto a long grass clearing near the shore, like planes landing at an airstrip on a busy day. The night was filled with calls and aerial displays unlike I had ever seen before.

The woodcock may also be seen in the daytime, but usually it's a fleeting glimpse. Often while walking a forest trail, I will unintentionally flush one from its cover. The bird will explode from the underbrush, with a whistling of wings, blur of feathers, and leaving me feeling as I've just had a heart attack. Their feathers range from brown and black, to gray and tan, and blend so well with the leaf litter that they perfectly camouflage with their surroundings. They do however, have an especially long bill, which they use to dig earthworms with. The stretched bill, large eyes, short legs, and stout body give the woodcock a comical look but serve it well for survival.

The woodcock has been known in the past as the whistling snipe, bog snipe, and, my favorite, the timberdoodle. I'm still researching that one! This upland game bird is still hunted by some, but probably best left in the sights of the camera or binoculars. Enjoy their ground and aerial displays as they invite you to dance the night away with them.

Let us probe the silent places,
let us seek what luck betide us;
Let us journey to a lonely land I know.
There's a whisper on the night wind,
there's a star agleam to guide us,
And the Wild is calling, calling...let us go.

~Robert Service

Little Dipper

Polaris (North Star)

Big Dipper

A Bear of a Star

Why does nature appeal to so many people? For one reason, it has so much to offer. Trees, flowers, frogs, insects, mammals, and birds, just to name a few, tap into the hearts and minds of folks and affect each one of us in a unique way. Also, nature is very tangible. The sights, sounds, smells, and textures create a feeling we remember and often seek to repeat. But what about the stars and constellations? They are a part of nature, yet seem to be in a different category. One that plays less on emotions and more on reason. Astronomers are scientific, logical, and calculated. Perhaps, or maybe stars are just intangible, out of reach, and part of the nighttime landscape we do not get enough of. Either way, I find the more I learn about and experience the night sky, the more I want to learn about and be part of the greatest show on Earth.

Now is the perfect time to get out and marvel in the late night, open air theater. The nights are cool, the bugs are still a month away, and the stars are bright. Actually, the brightness of the stars does not change over the seasons, rather cold air holds less water vapor, thus producing a clearer night sky in winter and early spring. I suggest heading out of town, away from the light pollution, finding a field or large body of water, and gazing upwards for familiar shapes.

Start with a constellation that has been a part of folklore throughout civilization - the Big Dipper. As a youth, it was the only one I new, or thought I new. The Big Dipper is made up of four stars that form a rectangular shaped cup and three stars forming a handle coming off the upper left side. Natives from America and Canada, along the Maritime Provinces tell a story in which the cup of the Big Dipper is the form of a bear and hunted each year marking the new season.

The Latin name for this set of stars is Ursa Major. Ursa is the Latin word for bear. The Greeks also had a bear story for this constellation, where a woman, Callisto was turned into a bear and her son Arcas, also became a bear, which in-turn became the Little Dipper. Arcas comes from the root word Arkitos – meaning bear in Greek. This is also where we get our word arctic from.

The Big Dipper has been called a plough, wagon, and even a bull's thigh by different cultures. One significant representation was to the slaves in the United States. They saw Ursa Major as a drinking gourd. Upon looking at the two outer stars of the "cup" one can follow a line through the two stars up to the last star on the "handle" of the Little Dipper. This infamous star is named Polaris or the North Star. Slaves seeking to escape north, by way of the Underground Railroad, would travel under the cover of night and use the North Star to guide their flight.

The stars have not really changed over the past 2,000 years and link us with stories to people and places that have come before us. The night sky is shared with millions of people every evening and connects us with past, present, and future generations. Don't wait for the next comet or meteor shower to venture out into the "final frontier." Rather, find a map and set your sights on the heavens above!

Happy Anniversary!

In May of 1995, wildlife biologists in the Chequamegon National Forest near Clam Lake, Wisconsin, released 25 elk into the wild and reintroduced a native species to the north woods. As a result of their efforts the elk herd is currently estimated at 103 and still growing.

Historically, elk have roamed the woodlands of Wisconsin, but with pressure from hunting and farming, elk were extirpated by 1886. An attempt to reintroduce elk failed in 1932, but with concentrated monitoring and research, the release in 1995 can now be called a success.

Intensive radio collaring of calves, cows, and bulls, have allowed researchers to monitor movements with radio telemetry. Information has been gathered regarding feeding habits, reproduction, dispersal, and survival rates. Threats to the elk's survival include vehicle collisions, predation, parasites, and accidents. Over the past ten years, 48 elk deaths have been reported.

Through public education, the elk herd has existed without too many problems. Increased warning areas have helped motorists avoid collisions, but threats still remain to calves, especially due to increased ATV activity around the area.

Elk are well suited for the extreme cold and snow of northern Wisconsin and are not affected by the high deer population. The Dept. of Natural Resources hopes to have the elk herd increase to 1,400 animals. The U.S. Forest Service plans to construct viewing platforms for the public within the national forest. The return of the elk to northern Wisconsin provides balance and beauty to the landscape, and we should be proud to call them neighbors.

Birds of a Feather

Whether you hike the trails or stay close to the backyard, you share something in common with millions of people around the country – birds. Birds are the most abundant observable wildlife in the world. Often taken for granted, birds provide us with enjoyment through their behaviors, colors, and songs. In fact, birding and bird products such as birdseed and birdhouses, account for the biggest hobby in time and money spent – more than any other pastime.

It may seem that bird watchers are eccentric folks always in search of rare sightings. Interestingly, many common everyday birds seem to always make a birder's "top ten" list. Birds such as the northern cardinal, black-capped chickadee, and American goldfinch, rank as favorites across the country.

These birds visit our feeders and fill the air with songs, and often become the friendly "regulars" we look forward to seeing everyday. I think it is better to see the same birds daily and learn their songs and behaviors, than to see a species once and never grow accustomed to their presence. And when asked my favorite bird? It is always the one I'm currently watching.

A Hike to Remember

Here's a question for you: What did you see today? What caused you to stop, if even for 10 seconds, and witness something in nature? Were there sightings of hummingbirds at your feeder, wildflowers in bloom, a squirrel's tenacity at getting in your bird seed, or was it a mother goose leading her goslings across a pond?

Could you imagine a day without seeing something in nature? Unfortunately, this is the case for many people. Often it seems that we are pulled farther and farther away from the natural world that surrounds us. The fabricated life of big business, mass media, entertainment, consumerism, and government politics, all conspire to keep us busy, bogged down, distracted, and on edge. Simply put - its information overload. The irony of it all, is that with so much information, folks are becoming increasingly disconnected daily with our planet and the *real* life around us.

I encourage everyone to continue to experience nature first hand and share with others the wonders you find. Perhaps a good 'ole nature hike is calling. I often comment that no two hikes are ever the same. Regardless of how many trips you make on the same trail, there is always something new to see. During springtime this is especially true. Every walk out the back door yields a new discovery. My records from past springs help me to anticipate what I may find over the next several months.

While on foot, we may uncover columbine, bunchberry, and wood betony in bloom. Fern fiddleheads are unfolding and damselflies are on the wing. Orange hawkweed and lupine will add color to your hike and white admiral butterflies will soon grace the air.

If you travel by canoe, look for dragonfly exoskeletons along shore line reeds. Listen for bullfrogs calling in June and look for fireflies to light your way. Don't forget to jot down your findings and keep a record to compare with for next year. Writing also helps you recall the birds and wildflowers you just identified. Take the time and make the next hike one to remember.

We live in a society that tries to diminish us to
the level of the ant heap so that we scurry mindlessly,
getting and consuming. It is essential to take
counteraction…Every one of us needs to be stretched
to live at our best, awakened out of dull moral habits,
shaken out of petty and trivial busy-work.

~Eugene Peterson

Continental Calling Card

What makes a good bird song? Strictly speaking, every bird song is a good song, but there are some that resonate more deeply within us than others. Perhaps it is the ease of recognition, like the *caw* of the crow and *ank, ank, ank,* of the nuthatch, that we gravitate towards. Maybe it is the lyrics we put to the rhythm of the call, such as the *who cooks for you, who cook for you all,* of the barred owl, or the *peter, peter, peter,* of the tufted titmouse, which aids our memory. Or is it the feeling that the call inspires within us, like the haunting cry of the common loon or the rattle of the sandhill crane? More likely, it is a combination of all three. Such is the case with a true icon of the northwoods: the white-throated sparrow.

The white-throated sparrow, *Zonotrichia albicollis,* may have been one of the first bird songs I learned when I came to the northwoods of Wisconsin. It certainly was not difficult to remember - for lyrics and stories were offered by bird enthusiasts to supplement my avian education. The song of the white-throated sparrow is described as a high, clear, lingering whistle. The call starts with two sharp, high notes, followed by three sets of staccato triplets. The common lyrics set to the rhythm are, *Old Sam, Peabody, Peabody, Peabody.* Of course, if you are across the boarder, with our friends to the north, the call is *Old sweet, Canada, Canada, Canada.*

I have also heard the sparrow referred to as the "Peverly bird," but only by real "old time" birders. The story goes that old farmer Peverly was out in his field one day, but could not decide on which crop to plant. From out of the bushes he heard a call telling him to plant wheat. The bird cried, *"Sow wheat, Peverly, Peverly, Peverly."* The rest is history.

The simple stories and interchangeable lyrics of the white-throated sparrow's song, make it a favorite of many and a popular companion while hiking, camping, and exploring the northwoods. In fact, the white-throated sparrow will sing well after sunset and into the night. One evening, while camping along the Brule River, I heard one singing at 11:30 pm. Not unusual for this strongly territorial bird. White-throats establish and defend their territory from others, and each bird has subtle variations within their song. Interestingly, some females get into the spirit by singing a few bars, thus protecting the "neighborhood." (Typically, only male songbirds "sing," with cardinals being another exception.)

White-throated sparrows return in late April and throughout May, from their winter whereabouts. From Texas to Florida, and even southeast Wisconsin, white-throats fly north and return to their breeding grounds. I typically find them in mixed or open coniferous forests, with dense shrubby undergrowth. Females build a small nest, close to, or on the ground, with grasses, twigs, needles, and lichen. After mating, the female generally lays 4 olive-sized eggs. After two weeks, the eggs hatch and young are fledged in 12-14 days.

White-throated sparrows eat a vegetarian diet consisting of grass and weed seeds, berries, and buds from maple, beech, and oak trees for most of the year. When their eggs hatch, the adults switch to eating insects and gobble up caterpillars, beetles, flies, and spiders, providing necessary protein for themselves and their young. Fledglings must avoid predators such as sharp-shinned hawks, kestrels, owls, and foxes, in their quest for survival.

I'd like to put the white-throated sparrow it its rightful place - with the loon, beaver, black bear, and white pine, as unforgettable icons and tenants of the north. Hopefully, locals and visitors alike,

71

will relish in the call of this spirited sparrow, and linger in the echoes of the song that defines a place like no other.

Three Times the Beauty

We all have heard the old saying, "leaves of three, let it be." This usually is said in context when referring to poison ivy, but is more appropriately applied when looking at the splendid large- flowered trillium. This showy, spring ephemeral can cover a forest floor and grab the attention of even the most casual outdoors person.

Large-flowered trillium, *Trillium grandiflorum,* takes its namesake from the Latin *tri* meaning three and *grandi* meaning large. Trilliums come in many different species in Wisconsin, but all have three leaves, three petal, and three sepals. In fact, early Christian settlers to North America referred to it as the "trinity flower." Easy to identify, large-flowered trillium blooms in May and June, with three large white petals set atop three green, large pointed sepals.

Trilliums prefer a moist, shaded habitat in which to grow. The rich soils of mixed hardwoods, containing aspen, oak, and maple, are the perfect home for large-flowered trilliums. At one time, Native Indian tribes and European settlers used trillium for medicinal purposes. Later, the flower was over-harvested by gardeners, which lead to legislation for the protection of the plant. One reason for the needed legal protection is the length of time required for reproduction. New trillium seeds, once germinated, take at least six years before developing the first blossom. Also, plants already established, when picked, may not produce enough sugar and starch for the bulb to produce a boom the following year.

Fortunately, large-flowered trilliums have an ally on their side. Ants often take trillium seeds back to their nests, where the larvae feed on the sticky coating. The seed is then discarded by the ants and in turn, distributed throughout the forest. We too can be an ally of the trillium - by not picking, harvesting, or damaging these debonair denizens of the forests, and by providing and protecting the habitats in which they are found. I encourage everyone to get out and enjoy the trilliums this spring and just like The Beatles sang, "Let it be."

Dive, Rattle, & Roll

If you have ever spent any time in a mall, and hopefully it's as little as possible, chances are pretty good you will see a small group of teenagers hanging out. Quite possible, there will be one within the group wearing a leather jacket, chains around the hips, and sporting a Mohawk haircut. Call it teenage angst, attention deficit (the need for attention), or simply marching to the beat of your own drum, it is hard not to notice this creature. And so it is when I am paddling my canoe down a calm river on an early Saturday morning. The sun is breaking through the trees, several painted turtles are basking on a fallen log, and a dragonfly has perched on my water bottle, when just a short distance up ahead, a vision drops from a tree, lets out a raucous rattle, and skirts the shoreline for 100 feet. If the bird world has a punk rocker, it must surely be the belted kingfisher.

The belted kingfisher, *Ceryle alcyon,* is common throughout North America and the only kingfisher species north of Texas. Other than terns, they are the only small bird that dive headlong into the water. It should be no surprise the belted kingfisher eats fish. But contrary to some misguided anglers, kingfishers take only small fish such as minnows and chubs, rather than large game fish. Belted kingfishers also eat frogs, crayfish, tadpoles, salamanders, insects, and mice. They can often be seen perched on the limb of a snag close to the water.

Almost any small or medium sized river will have a pair of belted kingfishers. They burrow into the side of the river bank and make a nest 3 to 6 feet into the earth. When paddlers come through, the birds fly ahead and wait, then fly ahead again, and finally double back on the other side of the shore. You can estimate their territory size by the distance from when you first see them, to the point at which they turn around and go back. It is approximated that the average breeding territory is 1,000 yards of shoreline.

Sightings are common and easy on a summer's day. Look for the large head, with crested feathers, atop a small, grayish-blue body, or simply listen for the rolling rattle as it flies. Both sexes have a gray band across the breast and females have an additional rusty orange band across the belly. Belted kingfishers are amazing to watch, especially as they hover above the water and dive into the aqueous buffet. Kingfishers take their prey to a tree limb and swallow it whole. Later, the bird will regurgitate the bones, much like an owl will do, leaving evidence of its presence.

Kingfishers are quite legendary. One story tells of the bird leaving Noah's ark and flying towards the sun, having its breast scorched and feathers changed to resemble the evening sky. Another comes from Greek mythology. Alcyone, from the sisters of Pleiades, and from whom the belted kingfisher derives its Latin name from, was grief stricken and threw herself into the sea and was then turned into a kingfisher called Halcyon. Halcyon now refers to calm and peaceful days in nature.

Whether it be by actions or by looks, the belted kingfisher has garnered the attention of both past and present generations. This big-headed bird is the perfect interruption on your canoe trip and provides an escorted journey along the waterways. Enjoy these likeable "punks" of nature – and all without the attitude!

In His hand is the life of
ever creature and the
breath of all mankind.
Job 12:10

SUMMER

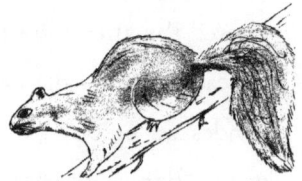

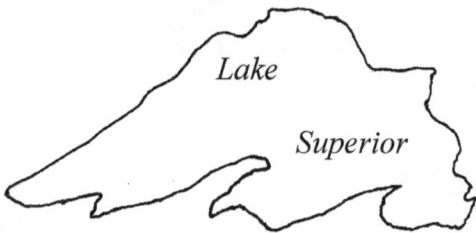

To see a world in a grain of sand

and Heaven in a wild flower,

hold infinity in the palm of your hand

and eternity in an hour.

~William Blake

Next Stop... Nature

Entrenched in the dog days of summer, I keep an eye out for the simple joys in nature. Watching a garter snake dart across the trail, following the flight of a monarch butterfly, or going wildflower watching, serve me well and kindle my fascination with the outdoors.

But heading out in the mid-day heat will yield a noticeable stillness in the landscape. Much like the frigid days of winter, the summer's heat will keep most critters hunkered down until the sun retreats to the west and the night sky emerges. The best time to glimpse a view of wildlife is between four and six in the morning, as many mammals make tracks back to their dens. Although birds and squirrels are active after sunrise, anyone venturing out after eleven o'clock a.m. will share the company of dragonflies, butterflies, and wildflowers. Whichever time of day you travel, there is something waiting to spark your curiosity and challenge your knowledge. Einstein once wrote, "Nature's mystery lies not in her cunning, but rather in her grandeur." I do believe he was right!

The Call of the Wild

Returning from the coastal waters of the Gulf of Mexico and the Atlantic Ocean, the common loon ventures north in early spring. The familiar tremolo, yodel, and wail calls can be heard throughout area lakes. For many, the distinctive, haunting cries of the loon represent the wildness of the northwoods.

The common loon, *Gavia immer,* searches for open water in the spring. Clear lakes with ample fish, reasonable depths to escape from predators, such as the eagle, and long enough to provide a "runway" for take offs, make suitable habitats. Most loon territories have multiple nesting sites found along the edge of the shore, and a nursery area for loon chicks to feed. The loosely constructed nests, made from the surrounding vegetation, are susceptible to heavy wakes from motorboats. Watch for the newly hatched loon chicks with downy feathers riding on the backs of their parents to avoid getting soaked and suffering from exposure.

Look for the dark head and checkered back of the loon on the bigger lakes of northern Wisconsin. The solid bones of the loon make them excellent divers, able to reach depths of 100 feet, but also require a long take off area to gain flight. Scan the area after a loon dives and watch for it to resurface. Loons, like many folks fond of the northwoods, return to the same lakes each year. Listen for this call of the wild and the sounds of the northland on your next hike around the lake this summer.

Shades of Gray

Squirrels have captured the attention of nature enthusiasts everywhere, and no squirrel has a more polarizing effect on folks than the gray squirrel. While some will go out of their way to feed these dashing darlings, others will spend countless hours trying to outwit the timber thieves. Just ask a neighbor or bring up the topic at work – and watch the fur fly.

The Eastern gray squirrel, *Scuirus carolinensis*, is found in the eastern half of the United States, from the Dakotas south to Texas, and east to the Atlantic Ocean. They are a gregarious game animal and important agent for distributing and planting seeds, many of which will grow into trees.

Gray squirrels are generally gray, but also come in black phases and occasionally are white or albino. The big bushy tail is the gray's signature trademark and uses it for balance, warmth, communication, and shade. From head to tail the gray squirrel can be 20 inches in length and weigh over 1 pound.

The speed and agility with which these rodents travel is easily seen on any given day. Gray squirrels are solitary by nature but are not overly territorial. Many will congregate in local parks or at bird feeders to amicably feast on the day's offering. But like most animals, when food is the issue, scuffles, scolding, and the inevitable chase will ensue. Actual fights are rare and the antagonistic behavior serves to establish social order.

The gray squirrel is a native of the hardwood forest and is also found in a mixed hardwood-coniferous woodland. Nut bearing trees, primarily oaks, are important for their diet. They also feast on buds, flowers, seeds, berries, mushrooms, insects, and the inner bark of trees. Acorns are buried throughout the gray squirrel's home range of 2-7 acres. A touch of the nose on the buried acorn will aid in retrieval as the gray will search out the treasure again during winter.

With much perseverance, and plenty of tasty treats, gray squirrels can be tamed and trained to your liking. If you wish to rid them from your bird feeders, there are many "squirrel proof" feeders on the market. But I would encourage folks, with all the imagination and creativity at their disposal, to try and outwit these spirited speedsters on their own. It's more fun that way, and besides, you might end up a member of the gray squirrel's fan club!

Bee ology 101

Social, busy, frightful, buzzing, honey, stings – all come to mind when the word "bees" are mentioned. Any insect that has the capability of stinging, holds a special place in our minds and tends to cloud our judgment. Perhaps for you, that is the case with the honey bee. I admit that until recently, I had only casual knowledge of the honey bee and much of that knowledge consisted of knowing to stay away from them. So, all the more reason to dive into the sticky world of the honey bee.

Honey bees fall into the order, Hymenoptera, which includes bumblebees, wasps, hornets, and yellow jackets. Without going into the specific classifications, i.e. sub-orders, family, etc., it is sufficed to say there are many differences between the aforementioned insects. One of the biggest, and for some, the most important difference, is in the fact that honey bees can only sting once - after which they die, whereas wasps, hornets, and yellow jackets can sting multiple times. But as we'll soon find out, honey bees rarely sting and are quite gentle.

Honey bees are social insects that live in large colonies called hives. Each bee has a specific role within the hive and the life of a bee, from birth until death, is very structured. Honey bees live in hollow trees or can be "kept" in wooden boxes called hive bodies. We often hear about swarms of bees. A swarm is simply a queen bee and all the workers that have outgrown their existing home and are in the process of finding a new one. New colonies are started this way. Swarms are tightly packed clusters, containing thousands of bees, all revolving around the queen. If you find a swarm near your home, don't panic – just call you local natural resources department and they can usually get in touch with a local bee keeper who can hive the swarm.

The world of bees revolves around the queen in the hive. A hive has only one queen and she lives for several years. The queen's only job is to lay eggs. But wait, how does a bee become a queen? It all starts with the egg. After determining the need for a new queen, the worker bees feed the larva a substance called royal jelly for five days. The cell is then capped and the new queen will emerge after a total of 16 days. Once the adult queen hatches, she will fly outside the hive and mate with many drones. Upon her return, she spends the rest of her life laying eggs. It is estimated that a productive queen can lay 200,000 fertilized eggs a year.

With so many eggs to look after and a hive to attend to – worker bees are needed to do a multitude of tasks. Workers bees, the smallest and most numerous of the bees within the hive, are non-reproducing females. Worker bee eggs take 21 days to emerge from their cells. After which, the tasks begin. A worker bee starts out by cleaning cells and feeding larvae. She also tends to the queen with feeding and comb building. Later, the worker will guard the hive entrance, and then finally become a forager. As a "field bee" she locates and brings back nectar and pollen to the hive. Worker bees live for about 35 days and a typical hive will have 50,000 adult worker bees.

Lastly, the hive consists of drones. Drones are male bees, whose sole job is to mate with the queen, although most never do, and the ones that successfully mate die right afterwards. Drones cannot gather nectar or pollen and live within the hive, being feed by worker bees. During the fall, drones are driven out of the hive to perish and all drone larvae removed. This seemingly heartless act ensures that food supplies within the hive are not wasted over the winter. During the spring the queen will lay unfertilized eggs that will develop 24 days later into drones.

The hive is an efficiently structured entity, and an example of the whole being greater than the sum of its part. Each bee plays an important role within the hive and contributes to the success of the colony.

A colony of bees is always changing. Eggs are hatched, cells are cleaned, combs are built, and pollen and honey stored. A healthy colony will expand and eventually out grow their home. A swarm will leave the hive to start a new colony and repeat the process. It's all very complicated, yet once you start to study "bee·ology" it becomes less mysterious. Thankfully, the equipment used to keep bees is basic and has changed little over the past century. Modern beekeeping has progressed a long way as we look back and try to uncork the history of the hive.

The art of beekeeping, officially called apiculture, dates back approximately five to seven thousand years when ancient tomb drawings illustrated primitive apiaries. Writings on bees appeared in 334 B.C. with observations and descriptions on hive maintenance. Throughout time, monasteries have been havens for beekeeping. Monks made hives from pottery, straw, and hollow logs. Hives were small and swarms were encouraged to populate empty hives. At the end of the season the colonies would be destroyed and honey removed.

The challenge was to devise a hive in which the honey could be removed without breaking the comb or killing the bees. In 1806, a Ukrainian named Peter Prokopovich developed a movable frame from which the bees could pass from chamber to chamber. Almost 200 years before this, honeybees had been introduced to North America, and the production of honey and wax became a lucrative business. In southern Wisconsin honey sold for 30 cents a gallon.

In 1851, Reverend Lorenzo Langstroth discovered the space needed between frames in which the bees would not build comb. This lead to the modern day movable frame and revolutionized honey extraction. Bees are now housed in wooden boxes with frames inside. Each frame can be removed and honey taken out without damaging the combs. This simple method is currently used today.

A bee hive consists of wooden boxes with rectangular frames inside. I remember as a child seeing hives and thinking they looked like small dressers. The bottom two or three boxes are called hive bodies. It is here, on the frames, where the queen lays eggs, brood is raised, and pollen and honey stored. The frames have a wax coating on which worker bees draw out comb. Combs are the individual cells, shaped like hexagons that form across the frame.

Above the hive bodies are slightly smaller boxes called supers. Supers are for storing extra honey, and can be taken off by bee keepers for harvesting. Supers contain 10 frames and each frame is put into an extractor, which spins and removes the honey through centrifugal force.

The entire unit sits on a bottom board with an entrance into the hive for the bees. Above the top super is an inner cover with an opening for the bees and for ventilation and finally, a telescoping cover fits over the very top for protection. The equipment is simple, yet genius in design.

Apiculture takes patience, basic knowledge, and wisdom - gained only through years of working with the bees. Perhaps that is why it appeals to so many people and continues to be a favorite pastime, hobby, and career throughout the world.

After a busy summer of work by the bees, a beekeeper can hope to harvest surplus honey stored in the supers. Depending on the weather conditions, morale of the hive, and attentiveness of the beekeeper, the liquid gold may be rewarded in abundance or simply enough to see the hive through the winter.

Before honey can be harvested, it must first be collected by field bees and brought back to the hive. Bees leave the hive in search of nectar. Flowering plants produce nectar and entice the bees to land on them. In turn, pollen is also collected on the bees and transferred from one plant to another. Bees fly back to the hive and transfer the nectar to worker bees, which then place the nectar in the combs. The nectar is mixed with enzymes and stored until the water inside evaporates and is down to about 17%. Finally the honey is capped over with wax and stored until needed.

Supers of honey can be removed from the hive when they are 80% full. Each frame is then uncapped by using a long knife to slice off the wax covering. The wax can be set aside to be used later in candle making. The uncapped frames are placed into an extractor. The extractor is spun - using centrifugal force to remove the honey, and then the contents are strained to remove any impurities. The strained honey is bottled and stored for future use and sale. It's as simple as that.

Honey, once called the nectar of the gods, was the world's first sweetener. Until the recent production of refined granulated sugar, (from sugar beets and sugar cane) honey was a staple in every baker's kitchen. Honey consists of mainly fructose and glucose carbohydrates. And unlike white sugar, it also contains a wide array of vitamins, minerals, and antioxidants. Honey purchased in the store contains no preservatives and is truly nature's perfect gift.

Honey can be found in a variety of forms. There is the common liquid honey, spun honey, and comb honey. Spun honey, also called whipped honey is a spreadable, finely crystallized form. Comb honey comes with the wax comb and all. Interestingly, pure honey will never spoil. It will however, over time, crystallize. A jar of crystallized honey can be placed in a pan of hot, but not boiling, water and will reliquify.

Honey can be substituted for sugar in almost any recipe. General guidelines for cooking with honey suggest substituting ¾ cup of honey for every 1 cup of sugar. Then reduce the total amount of other liquids in the recipe by ¼ cup per cup of honey. Finally, lower the baking temperature 25 degrees to prevent over browning. Experimenting with honey will add flavor to your cooking and conversation.

The amazing world of bees and the treasure they provide can be best summed up in the words Dick Paetkze wrote. "It is the soul of a field of flowers…and is a marvelous work of nature that makes the best factories of man look disorganized, lazy and of very little value. An expression of love and a special gift to man."

Sweet Flyer

Question: What is metallic-green on top, white underneath, has an iridescent red throat, is hyperactive, loves sweets, and goes zoom, zoom, zoom, all daylong? If you guessed the little kid down the block, you'd be close, but in reality – it's the ruby-throated hummingbird.

The ruby-throated hummingbird, *Archilochus colubris,* is the dynamo of the bird world. Averaging 1,000 heartbeats per minute in flight, and wings beating 75 times *per second,* we can begin to appreciate the velocity at which these birds live and their need for a high-octane diet. Many folks put out colored sugar water or a premixed nectar solution in backyard hummingbird feeders. Hummers feed 4-5 times per hour and the backyard buffets supplement their diet nicely. They continually search out nectar from flowers and also eat insects that provide them with protein. In fact, 25% of a hummingbird's diet is insects.

There are 25 different species of hummingbirds in the United States, but only the ruby-throated is typically found east of the Rocky Mountains. With only this species in the northwoods, identification is simple. The males are fun to watch as they defend their territory - often chasing away other males while engaging in a pendulum-like flight pattern. (Only males have the ruby-colored throat.) With such an active lifestyle, it's not often that I get to watch a hummer at rest, perched on a branch or wire along side the house.

Hummingbirds migrate south to Texas, cross the Gulf of Mexico, and spend the winter in Central America. During the fall,

87

many people see the birds at their feeders and worry if the allure of easy food will keep them from flying south. Ruby-throats fill up at backyard feeders along the journey, as they get ready for their non-stop flight over the Gulf. Instincts triggered by the amount of daylight, angle of the sun, and air temperature, compel the hummingbird to migrate south. Our feeders are simply filling stations along the way – self serve only!

Nighttime Reading

Some folks enjoy reading before bedtime. It is a relaxing way to end the day and enjoy quiet time before you slumber. Have you ever considered paging through a field guide before bed? Leafing through a guide and reading descriptions of frogs, birds, mammals, etc., is a great way to learn about nature, and also prepare yourself for the next outing. It is amazing how looking through a field guide will open your eyes to the natural world. On more than one occasion I have looked over a guide, and the very next time I was out hiking and exploring the guide topic, I was seeing new things never seen before and able to identify items with ease. This works great for topics such as birds, wildflowers, mushrooms, and constellations.

I am reminded of a quote by Henry David Thoreau, while he was exploring the Maine woods. " I was in just the frame of mind to see something wonderful, and this was a phenomenon adequate to my circumstances and expectation, and it put me on the alert to see more like it."

Beauty In Motion

Summer days spent outdoors are
sure to provide moments of pleasure.
As the wind gently blows, a vision of
beauty flutters by. Looking like something from the tropics - the
tiger swallowtail butterfly is a favorite among nature lovers
everywhere.

This large, robust butterfly takes to the sky in May and is seen
throughout the summer. Named for the black stripes on its yellow
body and long extensions on the hind wings, the tiger swallowtail,
Papilio canadensis, is easily recognized in the northwoods. Feeding
primarily on nectar, look for these butterflies on favorite foods
such as cherry blossoms, honeysuckle, lilacs, joe-pye weed, clover,
and of course milkweed.

Found in both deciduous and conifer forests, and along edges
and streams, the tiger swallowtail begins life as a small brown and
white caterpillar, often resembling bird droppings. As it matures,
the caterpillar turns green and has two orange "eyespots" and a
yellow band near the front of its body. The well-camouflaged
caterpillar spends time munching on leaves high in the treetops.
The larva turns brown before pupating, after which the chrysalis
hangs from a twig. From there it spends the winter.

After the tiger swallowtails are out, many often congregate on
wet soils, damp sand, or on wet gravel roads. This behavior is
called puddling and serves to provide minerals, nutrients, and water
for the butterflies to ingest. In addition, research reveals that the
males cluster together frequently and may be part of a social

89

hierarchy for mating privileges. The mid-morning hours are a great time to observe this behavior.

Tiger swallowtails are the perfect introduction to the hobby of butterfly watching. Once identified, you will notice these winged-beauties often. Butterfly watching is fun and rewarding. If interested in starting, I would suggest getting an area field guide for butterflies and a pair of binoculars. Watching where one lands, then zooming in with the binocs is a great way to observe them and see the necessary field marks for identification. A phenology flight chart is also an excellent reference to assist your knowledge of who's in flight. These "flutter-bys" put on a show like few other insects do.

PHENOLOGY FLIGHT CHART (of a *few* common butterflies)

SPECIES	MAR.	APRIL	MAY	JUNE	JULY	AUG.	SEPT.	OCT
Mourning Cloak	*	* * *	*	*	* *		* * *	*
Gray Comma	*	* * *	* *	* *	* * *	* *	*	* *
Spring Azure		*	* * *	* * *	* *			
Cabbage White			* *	* * *	* * *	* * *	* *	
Tiger Swallowtail			* *	* * *	* * *			
Painted Lady			* *	* * *	* * *	* * *	* * *	* *
Meadow Fritillary			* *	* * *	* * *	* * *	*	
Red Admiral			* *	* * *	* * *	* * *	* * *	* *
Orange Sulphur			*	* * *	* * *	* * *	*	
Monarch			*	* * *	* * *	* * *	* *	
Common Wood-Nymph				*	* * *	* *		

Butterfly Gardens

With over 200 species of butterflies in Wisconsin, attracting them to your yard and providing habitat with viewing opportunities can be a rewarding endeavor. Butterfly gardens are becoming popular additions to many landscapes and the keys to creating a successful one are basic.

1. Location: The best location is one which receives mid-morning sun through the mid-afternoon and a spot that provides viewing opportunities.

2. Plant perennial plants that provide excellent sources of nectar. Choose plants that will bloom at different times during the summer. Herbs will also attract butterflies.

3. Provide habitat for caterpillars. Oak, aspen, birch, box elder, milkweed, nettles, and parsley are popular plants for caterpillars.

4. Do not use insecticides. They will kill both the adult butterflies and larvae.

Here is a list of a few native plant species for your garden. Best wishes for a colorful year.

Common Name	Scientific Name	Sunlight	Blooming
Columbine	Aquilega canadensis	Full to partial	May-June
Blazing Star	Liatrus spp.	Full to partial	July-Sept.
Bonset	Eupatorium perfoliatum	Full to partial	July-Aug.
Butterfly Weed	Asclepias tuberosa	Full to partial	July-Aug.
Fireweed	Epilobium angustifolium	Full to partial	July-Aug.
Joe-Pye-Weed	Eupatorium purpureum	Full to partial	July-Sept.
Lupine	Lupinus perennis	Full	June-July
Purple Coneflower	Echinacea purpure	Full to partial	July-Aug.
Swamp Milkweed	Asclepias incarnata	Full to partial	June-Aug.
Wild Bergamot	Monarda fistula	Full	July-Aug.

The kiss of the sun for pardon,
The song of the birds for mirth,
One is nearer to God's heart in a garden
Than anywhere else on earth.
~Dorothy Frances Gurney

Who's Doing the Blooming?

Wildflowers play a vivid role during the summer in the northwoods. Both the carefully cultivated backyard varieties, along with the prairie and roadside species, provide the heavenly hues across our landscapes. The splashes of color catch our eye and attract the insects necessary for pollination.

By now, most of the spring ephemerals have gone to seed, leaving only their leaves as evidence of another spring season. Summer wildflowers have taken over the fields, prairies, and roadsides. Orange hawkweed, lupine, and ox-eye daisies are out in force. These flowers are typically found in dry habitats and enjoy full sunlight. As you walk along country roads and open forest trails, you will hear the bees and see the butterflies going from flower to flower in search of nectar. Most flowers radiate a strong scent and along with the bright colors, help guide the insects in.

Other flowers starting to bloom in mid-to-late summer are tansy, fireweed, black-eyed Susans, goldenrod, and St. Johnswort. Incidentally, flowers such as St. Johnswort, bellwort, and miterwort, all contain "wort" within the name, and "wort" simply means common. Wood sorrel is abundant (and the leaves are tasty too), as are evening primrose, milkweed, and red clover. Jewelweed, also known as "touch me not" can be found along wet ditches and trails. Look for the delicate orange "tube-like" flowers hanging from the stems. Jewelweed contains tiny seedpods along its stem and towards autumn, the pods will burst open if touched – hence the alternate name.

Venturing out on the water you will find pickerel weed, white and yellow water lily, and arrowhead. Dense patches of pickerel weed provide great hideouts for fish and muskrats. Large numbers of dragonflies will continue to emerge from their aqueous environment, existing as predaceous nymphs, climbing out upon a stem or reed to shed their exoskeleton. Once warmed up and dried off, they take flight to continue their search of insects to eat.

Summer wildflowers are enjoyable to see and most are easy to recognize. It is interesting to learn that many were commonly used to heal an assortment of ailments. Many folks still rely on the healing powers of plants such as St. Johnswort and wild bergamot. (Wild bergamot's oil is part of Earl Grey tea.) A walk along a prairie is the perfect setting to experience some of the summer's best. Prairies provide the perfect theater for witnessing the winds as they dance across the land, watching storms roll in, and getting lost in a sea of color.

Bird Talk

Birds are the most abundant and most observable wildlife we have. It is estimated that there are roughly 9,100 species of birds in the world. Birds not only play important roles in the environment, they have also permeated our vocabulary. Think how many common phrases or colloquialisms use bird imagery. Most of the familiar sayings tend to be more positive rather than negative. Birds generally have an overall positive image in our country, although some folks dislike a few species, usually because they see the species as a nuisance without realizing the benefits the birds bring. But that's just me squawking like a wet hen. I've listed a few below and hope you can add to the list.

The early bird gets the worm.

Birds of a feather flock together.

A bird in the hand is worth two in the bush.

That's just ducky.

As the crow flies.

Don't put all your eggs in one basket.

Get your ducks in a row.

That's a feather in your cap.

Give a hoot, don't pollute.

Acting like an ol' mother hen.

<u>Superior – The Name Says it All</u>

"The legend lives on from the Chippewa on down of the big lake they call Gitche Gumee…" These familiar opening words from the Gordon Lightfoot song, *The Wreck of the Edmund Fitzgerald*, painted an image and mood in the hearts of radio listeners across the country. The song became Lightfoot's biggest hit and made the Edmund Fitzgerald one of the most notorious shipwrecks of Lake Superior. But more than that, it pointed to something dark and powerful about the lake. The magnitude, beauty and power of *the* lake has never changed, and if you talk to folks living near by it, they'll all tell you the same – there is an allure about the lake, a powerful presence that is both comforting and mysterious.

Lake Superior is the world's largest fresh water lake. At the risk of boring you with numbers, let me throw some at you. Lake Superior covers almost 32,000 square miles. The deepest point is 1,279 feet down. The lake contains three quadrillion gallons of water and if you would like to drive around it on the Lake Superior Auto Circle Trail, it will take 1,300 miles. These numbers are staggering and hard to put into perspective, but all it takes is an hour on the shore. Standing, sitting, watching, and listening - you will feel the allure.

For me, the lake provides a perspective for my life. I can run around, here to there, busy with work, friends and all my little projects, and there sits Superior. Just as it has for the last thousands of years. The lake provides much needed humility in my life. Living next to something with such grandeur provides peace and lets me know that I am a part of something bigger. A very small part I realize daily. Recently, I canoed the south shore by Cornucopia to visit the sea caves. Even with the shore in sight, I felt the power of the lake and was humbled in its presence.

Even more difficult to grasp is the winter on Lake Superior. It *can* freeze over completely! Next winter call ahead, and then come up to drive across the ice road to Madeline Island. You'll never forget that drive. Many folks ask about lake effect snow from

Superior. If the winds are from the north and there is a temperature difference between the air and lake, then lake effect snow will occur. The snow belt is east of Ashland and over to Hurley. The south shore experiences the moderating effects of Superior. The fall weather stays a bit warmer and the spring weather stays a bit cooler because of the lake. This also contributes to songbirds and raptors staying in the area for the winter. It is no easy task predicting the weather in this neck of the woods!

I consider the awe of Lake Superior and its rugged beauty, the jewel of the upper mid-west. Whether it is a trip to the Apostle Islands, fishing along the mouth of the Brule, or visiting the sea caves during winter or summer, Lake Superior will fill your heart and mind with vivid images and memories you will never forget.

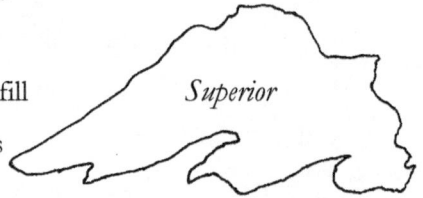

Superior

At the Hop

Ask any child to name a frog and invariably the response will be "bullfrog." With its impressive size and resonating sound, the bullfrog lays claim to the amphibian's most acclaimed star.

No question that kids and frogs go together. A lifetime of nature experiences may be rooted in the first frog encounter. Bullfrogs provide just enough accessibility and just enough squeamishness for any seven year old to take notice. After the first chorus of the low-pitched "brrr-rr-rumm" the hunt for the bullfrog officially begins.

Bullfrogs are the largest North American frogs, often reaching eight inches in length. Quite variable in color, these frogs can appear green, yellow, olive, or brown. Brownish spots may also be noticeable on the back. Bullfrogs have a conspicuous circular patch behind the eye. This spot, called the tympanum, serves as the ear membrane. A distinct ridge of skin runs from the eye and curves around the tympanum to the shoulder.

Besides the resounding bass call, bullfrogs are known for their jumping prowess. Leaps of 15 feet or more are common and used to escape predators such as raccoons, fish, snakes, turtles, herons, otters, mink, and humans. Fish are considered the biggest threat to the bullfrog tadpoles. These tadpoles require 2-3 years for development and will live in a permanent body of water until metamorphosis occurs.

Found throughout the country, bullfrogs are to summer lakes what corndogs are to state fairs. There is something irresistible about looking for bullfrogs, and if you're out with the kids, you just might find yourself knee deep off shore, laughing out loud, and holding up the prize in your hand.

Fountains of Youth

A walk across the prairie or down an old abandoned field is the perfect pastime for summer and nature lovers alike. One sure sign that summer has arrived is with the blooming of common milkweed. This tall, showy plant does it all – from providing nectar for the bees to aerial displays in fall, and of course, acting as nursemaids to millions of monarch butterflies each year.

97

Found in fields, along roads, clearings, and in backyards, common milkweed stands up to five feet tall and produces pinkish flower clusters, attracting bumblebees, honey bees, and butterflies to its fragrant blossoms. Milkweed gets its common name from the milky sap oozing out from broken leaves and stems. Most folks know milkweed for its relationship with monarch butterflies.

Monarchs migrate north from Mexico, arriving to the northwoods in late spring. Female monarchs deposit their eggs on the plant's leaves and when the eggs hatch, the tiny caterpillars feed exclusively on the milkweed. I enjoy finding and watching the green and yellow striped caterpillars day after day and seeing their rapid growth. After several weeks, the caterpillar will attach itself to the underside of a leaf and spin a cocoon, forming a chrysalis from which it will emerge as an adult butterfly.

Common milkweed develops large seed pods by the end of summer. According to *The Forager's Harvest* by Samuel Thayer, the young pods are actually edible. The seed pods grow rough and brittle and will break open during fall. Hundreds of seeds, attached to silky hairs are carried by the wind over the landscape to propel the next generation of milkweed. Interestingly, milkweed also sends root suckers out to advance its cause. In the late 1920's the silky seeds were used to stuff life vests.

Milkweed contains cardiac glycosides which have been historically used in medicine. Monarchs absorb the glycosides in their body and are toxic when eaten by predators. Just another example of how something as simple as common milkweed can reveal the connections in nature and relationships found throughout the wild. Whether as a host to the monarch caterpillar or as a bio-agent in the adult's defense, common milkweed plays an important role in nature while providing us an opportunity to watch a real fountain of youth.

Under Construction

The beaver has made historical, economical, and environmental impacts on North America. Often called nature's engineer, the beaver is found through the United States but is often associated with the northwoods.

The beaver, *Castor canadensis*, is the largest rodent in North America. It lives a semi-aquatic life, feeling safest from predators while in the water. The beaver can range from 45-60 pounds and can be 3-4 ft long, including their long tail. Beavers never stop growing their entire life.

The noticeable large front incisors of the beaver enable it to chew through trees and construct its lodge. Once logs, branches, and mud are piled up for a bank lodge, the beaver will simple chew its way in and create living space for its mate and several young beaver kits to spend the winter in.

Beavers are keystone species: their actions influence the environment and all species within that environment. The beneficial side of beaver dams are the raised water levels - creating wetlands for raccoons, frogs, otters, great blue herons, wood ducks, belted kingfishers, hooded mergansers, and muskrats.

The detrimental side of beaver construction is the resulting slow flow of water, warmer water temperatures, and less oxygen, harmful to some fish such as trout. There is also timber destruction along shorelines and flooded areas.

Still trapped today for the luxurious fur, the beaver is an influential mammal that can affect the quality of life for both humans and critters alike. So remember, in the northwoods, road construction is not the only type of construction causing detours.

Northwoods, USA

Every state has it. It is the part of the state that some folks pretend does not exist, some folks wait all year for their week to travel to, and some folks call home. It may be northern California, the Upper Peninsula of Michigan, the eastern coastline of Maine, or the foothills of West Virginia. For us, it is the northwoods of Wisconsin. The large tracts of public land, the small towns dotting the map, and the sense of simple, down-to-earth living – all share in the appeal of the northwoods.

So where does the northwoods start? Is it north of Hwy. 29? Does it start past Hwy. 8 or north of Hwy. 70? Perhaps it starts with a feeling, a need for adventure, room to roam and an opportunity to listen. Sounds of the north define the area as much as sights and smells. The call of a loon, chatter of a red squirrel, and the harmony of wind through white pines, leave an indelible image and impression upon us.

The small towns of northern Wisconsin play a vital role in our definition of the northwoods. Each one has a charm, character, and local eatery (serving the area's best fish fry), that sit like a jewel just off a county road. Most of the towns have a yearly festival celebrating everything from blueberries, Jackpine Savages, the Chequamegon Bay of Lake Superior, or simply the world's largest fish boil. Each town has a story and claim to fame. That's the appeal – to learn the history, the characters, and the folklore of these small communities.

Our experiences will vary from season to season, but a trip up north will almost always result in another trip up north. From the small towns to the state parks, pine forests and south shore of the big lake, the northwoods of Wisconsin provides an amazing array of both individual and shared experiences. I'll see you there!

Orange You Glad You're Here?

Throughout the spring and summer seasons wildflowers come and go. The majority of wildflowers blooming in early spring are white. The next batch of bloomers are typically yellow, after which, there are reds, blues, and finally towards late summer the pink and purples ones come into bloom. The colors serve to attract the insects needed to pollinate them and provide an esthetic landscape for us to enjoy. There is one color that I am particularly found of, although it represents only a few summer bloomers, and that is orange.

Orange wildflowers come into bloom during early and mid summer and it could be argued that some are more red or yellow than orange. Common orange wildflowers include hoary puccoon, jewelweed, Indian paintbrush, turk's cap lily, butterfly weed, and of course, hawkweed.

101

Orange hawkweed is a favorite wildflower of mine, and can be found in dry fields, along roads, and in pastures. Hawkweed takes its name from the erroneous belief that hawks ate the flower for improved vision. The plant also goes by the nickname of "devil's paintbrush" because the wildflower can fill a farmer's pasture and not be eaten by livestock.

Hawkweed has a tall, single, hairy stem standing a foot tall. Atop the stem sits many orange flower heads. These flower heads contains many little ray flowers that radiate from the center. The flowers open in the sunlight and close at night and on cloudy days.

The appeal of these wildflowers stem from the flower's yellow center surrounded by the bright orange rays. Tending to grow in large clusters, a roadside may be blanketed by these colorful creations, and on a windy day, they provide a showy spectacle as they dance among the daisies.

On your next walk, stop and take notice of the wildflowers and decide if you'd consider them weeds or bouquet worthy. Take note of the color and the time of the season. You'll be sure to find one that appeals to your senses and becomes a favorite for years to come.

One of the most attractive things about
the flowers is their beautiful reserve.
~Henry David Thoreau

Language of the Loon

As we head into the second half of the summer, loons are busy raising their chicks. Teaching the youngsters how to fish, support themselves, take-off, and fly, are all part of the August curriculum. Have you ever wondered how they learn the vocalizations loons use to communicate with others? It's probably through instincts and repetition that the language of the loon gets passed to the next generation. Anyone camped by a northwoods lake can testify to the unique chorus of these boisterous birds.

What do these cries communicate? Actually, the loon has four distinct calls – each conveying a specific message. *The wail* is used to communicate with loons over a long distance. It sounds like the howl of a wolf. *The tremolo* is the classic "haunting laughter" we hear. It is an alarm call, but also used as a social greeting when birds are in flight. *The yodel* is longer and more complex than the other calls. Males use the yodel to establish territory or scare away intruders. Finally, *the hoot* is a short, soft call used to "talk" with other loons and chicks in close proximity.

The biggest threats to loons right now are uneducated boaters and anglers. Boats produce a dangerous wake that damage loon nests, and chicks can be easily injured by hooks and lines carelessly left off shore. Loons are synonymous with the northwoods and represent a wildness that folks come in search of. The language of the loon is a universal tongue heard throughout time. Let's protect these creatures so the next generation can listen and be captivated by this call of the wild.

103

Creature of Habit

I have heard an old saying that goes, "if an acorn falls in the forest – an eagle will see it, a deer will hear it, and a bear will smell it." The black bear, *Ursus americanus*, not only has an incredible sense of smell but is quite literally an eating machine. From the time it awakens until the time it falls asleep, the black bear is either eating food or looking for food to eat.

The black bear is Wisconsin's largest omnivore – eating everything from plants, fruits, nuts, berries, insects, fish, and rodents, to any type of meat they can acquire. This large mammal is familiar to most with its glossy black fur, large five-toed paws, and reputation as an uninvited campground guest. Although the black bear can come in a variety of colors such as brown and cinnamon, most bears in northern Wisconsin tend to be black. It is solitary and shy, avoiding human contact, but also a creature of habit. The black bear will easily become a regular visitor to any food source. Anyone with a large bird feeder in his or her backyard may be able to attest to this.

Black bears mate in late June or July. The rest of the year the male is alone and will live in wooded areas and some grasslands, with a home range of approximately ten miles. Females may give birth to 2 or 3 cubs during the winter while in the den. Dens can be under overturned trees, shallow caves, hollow tree cavities, or in thick stands of conifers. Bears will enter their dens in late November and usually emerge once again during the beginning of April.

Black bears engage in a winter slumber called torpor. They are not true "hibernators" because their body temperature does not drop to a low level and their heartbeat and respiration remains steady. They do however sleep the winter away without eating or defecating. These robust creatures can be easily aroused, often waking up in a cantankerous state.

Upon encountering black bears, I have found them to be awe-inspiring yet timid creatures. They readily seek the shelter of tall grasses, thickets, and trees to avoid human interaction. As with all wildlife, a few exceptional reports of black bears harassing people will occur. Most are the result of misinformed or careless actions by visitors to state parks. Black bears are a curious, powerful presence in the northwoods. They simple need their space and our respect.

Live History

Once referred to as "King of the Northwoods," the white pine has the stuff legends are made of. *Pinus strobus,* the eastern white pine, once loomed tall over the northwoods and although never completely dominated the northern forests, its presence was such to propel fierce logging operations during the late 1800's.

The white pine could reach heights of 200 feet and 10 feet in diameter. Today, pines that tall are rare, being susceptible to high winds and disease, but a few "granddaddies" remain in the Brule River valley reaching upwards to 165 feet. Over the past 200 years, millions of board feet were harvested and sent down river to mills along the way by logging crews.

The lumber is valuable for building materials but the tree itself is important for eagle nesting. The large expanse of the white pine's crown is able to withstand the weight of a nest that, over the years, can weigh over a ton. Look across any lake up north and scan the tree line. The tallest tree will surely be a white pine.

White pines have needles in small clusters or bundles of five. In the sunlight, the white pine has a soft, lacy look, and the branches turn slightly upwards. Sitting under a white pine is peaceful and soothing. The wind blowing through the needles emit a simple *shssss* sound, like the waves receding on your favorite beach. Search out these giants and listen to the story they tell. History comes alive in the northwoods.

Now Playing: Summer

It happens every season, but more so with summer and winter. I'll be standing outside, focused on some little happening, and then it hits me – the season is half over! We are on the downside of summer, and before you can finish that canoe trip, flip that burger, and visit the county fair, it will slip away.

I always need a month to warm up to the season. Acclimate, if you will, to the warm weather, the wardrobe change, the bugs, the traffic, and the tourists. More and more, it seems the summer comes on strong. It is not unusual to have 80°F temperatures in

May. By June it can be humid and once July hits – let the sweating begin.

The roads are full of trailered boats and the local drive-in eateries open for the season. Every town has a weekend festival, complete with flea market, farmers market, and parade. They celebrate the town, the heritage, fruits, berries, lumberjacks, or anything they can lay claim to. Sometimes I have no idea what they are all worked up about. I guess any reason is a good reason to fill main street with local wares, crafts, and food stands.

For me, summer means a trip to the Apostle Islands. A walk back in time, to physically remove myself from the mainland, and go to a place where visitors have gone for the past 100 years to relax and enjoy the tranquility of the islands. Families from Chicago, Milwaukee, Minneapolis, and as far away as Nebraska, routinely made the trek to Madeline Island and to the little town of La Pointe. Was it the island or was it the lure of Lake Superior that brought them back year after year?

This year's journey had a stop in Bayfield and to the Big Top Chautauqua. A hot summer night, listening to the music and stories under the tent, is always a highlight of the season. Now is the time I start reviewing my mental checklist. Have I camped and canoed enough? Have I explored someplace new? Have I grilled enough brats, ate plenty of potato salad, and sat out under the stars long enough to satisfy my soul?

I must wrestle with these questions and remember that the quality of experiences outweighs the quantity. I also realize the diminishing number of dragonflies, butterflies, and frogs, which lend themselves to the summer ambiance, are in need of attention. The late summer wildflowers are starting to peak and clamor in the wind to be noticed. And there is a white pine tree somewhere that needs to be napped under.

Without much fanfare, I'll set my course and plan my days - to soak up the season and let the summer wash over me. I'll walk the trails and country roads, slow my pace, set my anchor, and allow each moment to pass, raptured in the scenery I find within. Summer, with all its glory is here today, and there will never be another summer like this one again.

Curious Quarters

Most all of us enjoy the creature comforts of home. It is the place where we can relax, feel secure, and keep a few personal treasures. Have you ever imagined the homes of wildlife? Since no creatures are active 24 hours a day, they all must have a place to rest, roost, raise their young, den, dine, or bed down for a while. The varieties of "homes" are amazing and are unique as the creatures that use them. Let's turn back the covers and unearth some wild dwellings.

The Damp Domicile

Insects run the gamut for using interesting homes, and the spittlebug earns the blue ribbon for its creative condo. This tiny jumping insect lives on grasses, meadow plants, and wildflowers, where it sucks juice from the host plant, then surrounds itself with frothy white foam. The bubbly secretion is a mix of abdominal extract and air. After molting, the spittlebug nymph emerges as an adult froghopper - the minute, oval, brownish bug that land on us while walking around grassy areas. Look for this damp domicile on your next walk.

Colorful Cottage

Home truly is where the heart is, when it comes to painted turtles. These aquatic reptiles carry their home on their back, as the shell is the most distinctive characteristic of the turtle. The shell is made up of 60 different bones! The top of the shell is called the carapace and the bottom is called the plastron. Together they are fused by "bridges" and act as a protective armor to thwart predators. Whether in marshes, ponds, shallow bays, or backwaters of rivers, the painted turtle finds comfort by simply tucking into its shell and resting among the muddy waters and aquatic plants.

Lumber Lodge

The northwoods is weekend getaway for many city folks. Cabin lined lakeshores and waterways flow with peace and tranquility. One mammal that always has a scenic vista right outside its door is the beaver. It is no secret that beavers built lodges and dams. The fascinating part is the method. Beavers pile wood along banks of small lakes, rivers, and streams, from aspen and birch trees, and congeal it together with mud and clay. After a large mound has formed, the beaver simply chews its way in and creates a home for the family. The lodge usually has several

109

chambers for living space and food storage, with multiple exits. A lodge typically houses two adults and 2-4 kits. North America's largest rodent has cornered the market on wild construction.

Golden Castle

Walk the edge of any forest, field, or prairie, and you'll be sure to find goldenrod. Looking at the stem, you may see a ping-pong size growth halfway up. The circular "tumor" is called a gall, and plays host to a few different insects. It all starts when a female gallfly, tiny wasp, midge, or aphid, lays an egg on the goldenrod stem. A larva hatches and burrows into the stem. The plant responds to the intruder by producing tissue to heal the wound, thus creating the round gall in which the larva will live. Most larvae will spend the winter inside the gall, then chew their way out next spring. Check out a gall on your next walk: if the hole is straight, narrow, and flush with the edge, the larva made it out. If the hole is conical and looks like a mini crater, chances are a woodpecker or chickadee had a larva lunch.

Airy Abode

Colonial insects prefer large hives, and few are as stunning as the oval headquarters of the hornet. The hornet is a true recycler. It chews on wood fibers, mixing it with saliva, and produces a pulp from which it constructs the hive. The gray, flakey walls protect the hornets and provide chambers for their larvae. Construction continues throughout the summer as the colony grows, creating a spectacular sphere of shelter. After the hive is vacated in late fall, the winds, rain, and snow will breakdown the hive. The remnants may be used by other critters for nesting material. Nothing goes to waste in the wild.

Scenic Chalet

In late autumn, after the braches have let go of their leaves, many tree nests are revealed. One common nest I see is the leafy nest of the gray squirrel. In addition to tree cavities, leaf nests called "drays" are a popular dwelling for squirrels. The nests look worn and raggedy, precariously perched in the crotch of a tree branch, but provide shelter and warmth throughout the year. Squirrels do not hibernate and will stay in the nests during extreme winter weather. Made of twigs, leaves, and bark, drays provide safety for the newborns and cozy quarters on cold, wet days. This four-season chalet is sure to keep the squirrels from going nuts.

Most of the luxuries and many of the so-called comforts of life are not only not indispensable, but positive hindrances to the elevation of mankind. A man is rich in proportion to the number of things he can afford to let alone.

~Henry David Thoreau

Red and Resourceful

Once described as clever, cunning, and crafty, it could be just as easily stated as intelligent, elusive, and resourceful. The red fox, *Vulpes vulpes,* is a native to the northwoods and a gregarious guest on Isle Royale. As a member of the canine family, shared with wolves, coyotes, and dogs, foxes have long been the subject of folklore, children's fairytales and legends across world cultures and throughout times past.

The red fox has reddish fur, a large bushy tail, black tipped ears, and whitish color on the throat, underside, and tip of the tail. As a nocturnal hunter, we seldom get to watch this shy mammal. Foxes are solitary animals, except during breeding season. The female will usually have a den, with multiple entrances, often under a large fallen tree or beneath rock formations. Pairs will mate in January and the female will have four to six kits by April. Parents will hunt and supply food for the young and at nine months of age, the new foxes are fully grown.

The diversified diet and ability to live in a variety of habitats has allowed the fox to increase in numbers. I have seen red fox in mixed hardwood forests, along fields, rolling hillsides, and on the outskirts of communities. They eat everything from rabbits, squirrels, game birds, and snakes, to fruits, berries, and insects. However, it is mice and voles that make up a large percentage of their diet, often making them appear more cat-like as they pounce upon their prey.

Foxes have excellent vision, a strong sense of smell, and acute hearing that helps to locate food. The foxes on Isle Royal have become accustomed to campers and have lost the fear of humans. They associate people with food and have been known to make off with unattended snacks, gloves, and the occasional boot.

Sometimes labeled as a poultry predator or hen house raider, the fox is simply doing what comes natural. We need to be responsible for providing secure shelters for such livestock. Foxes are still hunted for sport and trapped for their fur; yet continue to maintain level populations. These sly, graceful animals are a joy to witness and share a moment with – a welcomed sight after a long days hike.

Summertime in a Bottle

Summertime quickly comes and goes as memories are made. Some memories are tightly held onto and some are let go of, fading into a distant blur. Souvenir shops tap into this phenomenon by associating material goods with emotional experiences.

The scene is all too common: you've just got off the ferry in Bayfield, returning from Madeline Island, after having a wonderful day in LaPoint. The irresistible urge to stop at a shop and pick up a t-shirt, hat, or other souvenir gift overtakes you. Why? I believe the chosen item represents a tangible record of our emotional experience. What if you could bottle an experience and literally drink it down? Thanks to staghorn sumac, now you can!

The staghorn sumac is a common little tree growing in backyards, along trails, and edges of old farm fields. At the end of the branches, large cone-shaped clusters of flowers bloom in July,

113

then soon turn into red berries. The berries are covered with tiny crimson hairs that are velvety to touch. The fuzzy hairs are reminiscent of the velvet covering on deer antlers, lending to the name "staghorn" sumac.

The clusters of berries can be collected in the fall and turned into a delicious summertime drink. Simply rinse and break open the berries in *cold* water while gently rubbing the hairs off – collecting the water and all the parts in a pan or bowl. Next, pour the contents through a coffee filter or fine mesh strainer then into a pitcher. This should remove the hairs and remaining "floaters." Finally, add sugar and sweeten to your taste. I prefer a more tart lemonade so I add less sugar. Chill for several hours. A refreshing beverage of summertime awaits.

Sumac tea can also be frozen and later enjoyed during the middle of winter, when cabin fever has flared up. (Make sure the container will account for the expanding liquids.) Whether it is late summer or the chilly days of winter, sumac tea reminds me of summer scenes and refreshing seasons still to come.

Nature's Fortune Teller

One of my favorite summer activities is to walk along trails and old country roads and see how many wildflowers I can identify. Amazingly, roadsides and other "disturbed" places make great homes for quite a few flowering friends. One summer wildflower that never fails to appear is the ox-eye daisy.

Oxeye daisy, *Chrysanthemum leucanthemum*, has a colorful past. Introduced into America and named after the European species which opened and closed accordingly from day to night, the daisy literally means the "day's eye." Not fondly thought of by farmers, daisies establish a stronghold on many fields and pastures. They can reproduce through underground stems and tolerate poor soil and dry weather conditions. Cutting the flower seems to only encourage new growth. Farmers also disliked daisies because they were thought to produce an unwanted flavor in milk if eaten by cows.

The large flower heads, with white petals (more accurately called rays), surrounding a yellow center, can be seen throughout much of North America, blooming from June to August. The oxeye daisy contains the chemical pyrethrum, which causes many insects to avoid the plant. A common favorite of many, the daisy is especially popular with the love struck. Many a suitor's fate lay in the outcome of "he loves me, he loves me not," as the last white petal is plucked from the flower.

The oxeye daisy, along with black-eyed Susans, common milkweed, and orange hawkweed, remain as wildflower staples throughout prairies and along back roads everywhere. The frequency and quantity serve to remind me of the graceful resilience found in nature.

115

Moonlight Memories

Summer nights often yield great treasures; whether it is camping, star gazing, or sitting with a friend by a fire, we recall these events fondly. Elements creating these vivid memories are the people, smell of campfire smoke, the summer breeze, and of course - the bugs! Mosquito's not-with-standing, most nighttime insects actually provide a pleasant evening atmosphere. Crickets, cicadas, and katydids, perform the summer soundtrack for the night sky. However, there are two "quiet" insects that bring just as much pleasure – the luna moth and firefly.

The luna moth, *Actias luna,* seen on warm summer nights, often attracted to bright lights, is one of the largest silkworm moths. Named after the Roman mythological moon goddess, the luna has pale-green wings measuring up to 4½ inches across and a long "tail" on each hind wing. In addition, the luna, like most moths from the giant silkworm family Saturniidae, has eyespots on all four wings. The silvery eyespots may serve as a defense system, giving the luna a much larger appearance to potential predators, while they fly through the night.

Native to North America and found only in the eastern half of the United States and southeastern Canada, luna moths start life as large green caterpillars having a yellow line running along both sides, and red or orange tubercles (short, round knobs) on the back. The larvae spend their days eating leaves of nut-bearing trees such as hickory, butternut, and walnut, but will also visit maple, birch, and oak. Upon reaching approximately three inches long, the luna caterpillar will wrap up in a leaf, spin a silky cocoon, and fall to the forest floor. There it will spend the winter protected from the cold by the insulating snow and its body's own anti-freeze.

Depending on the geographic location and weather, sometime in spring the adult luna moth emerges from the cocoon and sets off to find a mate. In the north woods, this usually takes place in June. The lifespan of an adult is short – several days to a week, with the next generation hanging in the balance. Luna moths have reduced mouthparts and do not eat during their adult lives. Males search out and follow the enticing scent given off by the females. After mating, females lay eggs on deciduous trees and then soon die. The eggs will later hatch and the new offspring will continue this cycle of life.

A popular moth with bug enthusiasts, the luna moth creates a vision that is not-easily forgotten in the summer night sky. The moonlit dance of the luna has captured the imagination of people both past and present, as they were once thought of as the souls of lost ones in search of light.

Another nighttime insect that has found a friendly niche in the hearts of children and adults everywhere is the firefly. As a member of the beetle family, there are over 130 different species of fireflies, each flashing its own rhythm of light as a way to communicate with a potential mate. Many children enjoy chasing these lightning bugs around the backyard.

On warm evenings in June and July, male lightning bugs take to the air and put forth a pattern of greenish yellow flashes. Females of the same species, usually resting on the grass, receive the signals. The females then respond with a series of flashes, after which a rendezvous may take place. The colorful communication process is possible thanks to the chemical compound luciferin found within the firefly. It reacts with oxygen in the bug's abdomen to emit the flashes. Interestingly, some females have the ability to send flashes of other, smaller firefly species, thus luring males in to be eaten!

After the eggs hatch, the larvae eat worms and snails, then hibernate in the ground during winter. Late in spring, they emerge as adults and soon seek out a mate, usually in meadows, wetlands, and moist open forests. Most adult fireflies are black or brown with a yellow, orange, or red trim, and blend well in their environment. Like the luna moth and firefly, we share an inherent attraction to light, each stepping to our own rhythm. Look for these unforgettable denizens of the dark on your next summer night stroll.

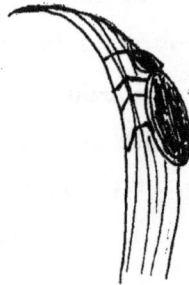

To sit and be still
To welcome the peace,
Hear the wind and movement of the leaves.
To watch with wonder
See the strains,
Watching revealed textures of the rain.
Follow a bird
To the tops of the trees,
From the smallest breath –all are free.
Is a simple act
Not hard to find,
The price is right, the cost is time.

FALL

big toothed aspen

quaking aspen

The plants and animals with whom we live teach us
about birth, growth, maturation, and death,
about the need for gentle care, and especially
about the importance of patience and hope.

~Henri Nouwen

Change...will do you good

Nature speaks a language all its own. It is talk of time and change. The former slow and steady, while the later can be predictable, unexpected, or sudden. Change can also be slow, like the decomposition of a fallen tree, constant, like the renewing of spring flowers on the forest floor, or sudden, like the upheaval of a pine tree in a windstorm. All have a purpose and all are a natural part of the cycles played out in wilderness.

The harvest moon approaches, rising in September. Can it be that the first frost, v-formations of honking geese, and hillsides draped in reds, yellows, and oranges are on their way too? Autumn is a spectacular season of change. I feel the most reflective during this time of the year. Perhaps I'm reflecting on the "harvest" of the past nine months or maybe it is a new perspective I see, looking through the stark branches of aspen and maple. Happily, I embrace this season with all the fervor of fledglings entering their first migratory flight.

Fall is a time to clean up the feeders, wrap up the garden, and patch that little mouse hole in the shed. These next months are for

121

taking long walks in the forest, biking through the arboretum, and sitting by a campfire at night. I don't mind retiring the summer wardrobe, donning the first sweatshirt, and feeling that first cold rain. No, here in the northwoods, being outside and taking part in the most colorful season of change is its own reward.

A Second Spring

Fall is fast approaching as I look forward to mild temperatures, cool breezes, and brilliant hues across the landscape. I can get caught up in the obvious changes and fail to notice the abundant activity surrounding me. September and October are just as busy as April and May. Could it be that autumn is really a second spring?

Mass migration is under way. The northland is blessed with two major migration observatories. Hawk Ridge in Duluth, MN and Whitefish Point near Sault Ste. Marie, MI are both excellent places to view bird migration, especially raptors. Birds will be heading south to California, Texas, Florida, and Central and South America. In addition, some bats and butterflies will depart the northland for warmer climates. Monarchs fly to Mexico for the winter, and in spring the next generation will return north.

Autumn wildflowers bring color, and hum with bumblebees along roadsides and prairies. Asters continue to bloom and goldenrods attract insects with bright yellows and mild fragrances. Mourning cloaks, eastern commas, and clouded sulfurs continue their flights well into October. Clouded sulfurs are the common yellow butterflies, with black boarders on the wings, we see along country roads and trails. Not to be outdone, the yellow-legged meadowhawk dragonfly has a later flight period – cruising into November.

Goldfinches nest in late summer and are now busy raising their recently hatched young. I have watched as goldfinches tear into large thistles, extracting their favorite food – thistle seed. A second litter of gray squirrels may emerge and collect fallen oak acorns to eat now and bury for later.

A second spring would not be complete without the scent of love in the air. Both porcupines and moose mate in the fall, each having long gestation periods. A porcupine carries the developing "porky" 210 days, while moose will carry their young a whopping 240 days! Both generally give birth to one baby during the following month of May.

With all this activity, it is easy to understand why autumn is a favorite time for many. Forests bursting with color, crisp northerly winds, and gardens yielding their harvest, all add to this special time of year. The only thing left to do...pull out my favorite flannel shirt, hit the trail, and witness the fall flurry. The second spring has arrived!

Prickly Pals

Existing almost unfettered in the northwoods, having a meal at every turn, and taking life at the speed of leisure, the porcupine is one of my favorite mammals. Having the opportunity to experience these creatures up close and marvel at their ways, I take great enjoyment in observing them.

The porcupine, *Erithizon dorsatum*, affectionately called "porky," is common to the northwoods and has literally carved (or eaten) out a niche on the landscape. Weighing 10-20 lbs., porkies waddle their way through life without too many cares. Days are spent slumbering in trees or occasionally browsing twigs of aspen, ash, or maple trees. Nights become active as the porcupine views the entire forest as his or her personal buffet. They will eat everything from buds, catkins, leaves, and twigs, to the inner bark and needles of almost every tree in the forest. I often notice large patches of missing bark on conifer trees that have been gnawed off – a telltale sign of a porky.

Porkies live in den trees and do not hibernate during winter. Active on most winter days, their tracks are easily seen in the snow, with footprints in a mild zigzag pattern and tail drag down the center. Den trees may have a hollow opening at the base and are filled with piles of scat. The comma shaped droppings, about the size of a large jellybean, are tannish brown, fibrous, and have a strong pine smell.

Probably best known for their quills, the porcupine's defense system is second to none. Predators need only attack a porky once to learn the valuable lesson – quills hurt! Contrary to some misinformation out there, porkies cannot shoot their quills, but rather the quills are dislodged from their bodies when a predator comes in contact with them, and often from a whack of the porkie's tail. The quills have tiny barbs on the ends and once imbedding into the skin, work their way in deeper over time. The porcupine's only predator is the fisher. A member of the weasel family, the fisher has the quick strike ability to attack the porkie's face, killing it, and then dining on the quill-free underside.

Relying on their sense of smell and touch, porcupines have poor eyesight and are common victims of road kill during the spring. Fortunately, these one-of-a-kind herbivores continue to thrive throughout the northland. Foresters may bristle a bit at their presence, but any tree damage a porcupine does can be seen in the light of providing the forest with more snag trees – a necessary component for wildlife feeding, nesting, preening, and perching sites. Songbirds, owls, mammals, and amphibians can partially thank the porcupine for the altered landscapes.

Migration Elation

Bird migration is under full swing right now. Many birds have long since departed for southern comforts, while some are just getting started. Birds have the daunting task of bulking up for the long journey south. Some flocks will stop at backyard feeders and other will not.

A large percentage of migrants travel at night. These typically include songbirds. Birds use light, which triggers migratory instincts, to navigate. The position and angle of the sun determines the departure date, while constellations assist in the navigation. Birds can be disoriented by light pollution from large cities and some will crash into tall skyscrapers.

Some migrants, such as hawks and water fowl, travel during the day. These are more easily witnessed, as with the example of

Canadian geese flying in their "v" formation. Many species of hawks are seen in abundance at Duluth's Hawk Ridge. Strong northerly winds will produce thousands of sightings on a clear day in the fall.

Be sure to watch for large flocks of snow buntings in late October. These small sparrows appear along roadsides, gravel pits, and weedy fields, often staying around for several days. Hard to spot on the ground, snow buntings blend in well with their surroundings with rusty streaks from head to tail. Once disturbed, they fly up a short distance and reveal their white wing patches and underside, before settling back down. Just another of the enjoyable, simple pleasures of the season.

Island Wilderness

Rising from the chilled waters of Lake Superior, Isle Royale National Park sits like a lost jewel, surrounded by isolation and miles from nowhere. The 45-mile long island, the largest of any in the Great Lakes, officially belonging to Michigan, became a national park in 1931. With over 571,000 acres, this rugged wilderness has changed little over the past two centuries. No roads, no cars, no shops, and but for one lodge at the east end for the tender foot, Isle Royale is an opportunity to lose yourself in nature. Without ever having been to Alaska, but from talking to friends that have, I venture to say that this is the closest one can get to a true wilderness experience without going north to the land of the midnight sun.

The island is open from May to October, closed the rest of the year, and accessible only by ferry or seaplane. The two or three hour boat ride, from ports in northern Minnesota and the Upper Peninsula of Michigan, allows a person a chance to be still, decompress from their daily routine, and await an experience they will never forget. Once on the island, surrounded by white pine, spruce, maple, and birch, one is quickly captivated by the enveloping forest, and the hiking trails that traverse them tell stories written by seasons past - each having a character all its own.

Isle Royale is known for its wildlife, most notably wolf and moose. The wolves roam free but are seldom seen, whereas the moose are abundant and found throughout the island. Fox, squirrel, beaver, and birds are common to the park. Both blue and gray jays are on the island and belong to the family **Corvidae,** which includes crows and magpies. Gray jays, also called Canada jays, are ubiquitous throughout the northern coniferous forest and become quite tame around campsites. I could not resist hand feeding one a peanut. These birds are highly intelligent, gregarious, and have a varied diet.

Visiting Isle Royale during the bookends of the season ensures the most solitude. Folks come from all over the country and the world, to be a part of this landscape, challenge oneself, and to experience a place where nature sets the pace, tone, and mood of the day. To wait as a female moose blocks the trail for her calf to cross, to hike to a remote campsite while the blowing snow obscures your vision, and to lie down and share the stars with a loon on the lake – is to know a peace and freedom that transcends time. This national treasure is truly wild.

Stoic Solace

To say that humans are ethnocentric would be an understatement. I could also say we are self-absorbed, self-centered, and often lacking in humility. Fortunately, this condition changes quickly once on Isle Royale – thanks to the moose! The largest member of the deer family reminds us we take a back seat to the natural history played out on the island.

Moose, *Alces alces*, are large hoofed mammals that roam freely throughout Canada, Alaska, and parts of Montana, Wyoming, and Michigan's Isle Royale. They are over 6 feet in height and males can weigh up to 1200 lbs. Fur color is dark, generally brown but often black, with a strip of dewlap skin (called "the bell") hanging six to ten inches from the underside of the throat. It has a massive head, large snout, and males sport large antlers from summer until December or January, after which they are shed.

Moose seem truly indifferent to the presence of people, intent on spending their days browsing leaves off trees and shrubs. Periods of highest activity are dusk and dawn, making them more crepuscular than nocturnal, although, like many mammals, there is some activity during both night and day. Moose tend to live in forests with a close proximity to water. Lakes, bogs, and swamps are sought out for cooling purposes and to browse on the aquatic vegetation.

Willow, mountain maple, sugar maple, ash, birches, and beaked hazel comprise much of the moose's terrestrial diet. Once the weather cools down and the leaves drop from the trees, moose may be found in the high country feeding upon balsam fir and seeking shelter in mature, dense conifer stands. Adult moose require 50 pounds of food a day. The impact of their browsing can devastate an area, with no shrub and reachable tree left untouched.

The rut starts in September lasting through October. During this period, male bull moose search out the female cows. Bulls are seen trudging amongst the forest, letting out low bellows and heavy grunts. Clashes between competing bulls will occur and the sparring can last for hours. Bulls jostle back and forth, locking antlers, pushing one another back. Younger bulls, 4 to 5 year olds, stand little chance against the older bulls. The display rarely results in serious injury, but bulls are said to be unpredictable and ornery during this period.

After mating, the female has a gestation time of 240 days. This is the longest of any mammal in the northwoods that does not include delayed implantation. (Delayed implantation is the process some animals are created with in which the egg is fertilized but not implanted into the uterus until a later date.) Cows usually give birth to one calf, although twins are not uncommon, and are highly protective. The calf will spend the next year with its mother and considered full-grown after 18 months.

Moose are primarily solitary but will tolerate small groups of three and four. Adult bull moose have no natural predators. Gray wolves prey upon the young, weak, and sick members of the species, but are no match for a full-grown bull. Shed antlers are a testimony to the armor and defense of the bull.

Truly northwoods creatures, moose seek the colder climates and enjoy wading in the icy bays of Lake Superior. These stoic statesmen and stateswomen of the north dictate the pace and quality of life for fellow inhabitants both big and small, and provide esthetic value to both landscape and observer alike.

Holidays and Homecomings

The next several months provide the perfect opportunity to celebrate the creations of nature as the landscape transitions from autumn into winter. Thanksgiving would not be complete without giving thanks for the wildlife we see daily. November is a good month to put up a bird feeder and provide the year-round residents a snack of seeds. I've noticed my feeders have been quite active lately. Chickadees, which have been intermittent visitors this summer, are now welcomed regulars to the backyard. Along with nuthatches, house finches, goldfinches (sporting their winter plumage), and red-bellied and downy woodpeckers, the birds breathe life into an otherwise homogenous backyard scene.

The cool months before winter sets in are perfect for getting out and bird watching. With many species already dispersed south, the identification process becomes simple. In fact, there is one bird you may be able to pick out blindfolded. The soft tapping and gentle *pik* call are both clues to the presence of the downy woodpecker.

The downy woodpecker, *Picoides pubescens*, is the smallest and most common woodpecker in the area. Downy woodpeckers are the attractive black and white birds found in open woodlands, parks, and backyards. Males have a red patch on the back of their heads, and at only 5 inches in length, these mini-excavators often move from tree to tree unnoticed.

I often hear these woodpeckers before I see them. Downy's let out a soft *pik* call, repeated several times a minute. They also have a "whinny" call, which descends in pitch towards the end. In an effort to find bugs to eat, woodpeckers tap holes into trees. The downy has a slow rhythmic tap. It occasionally will drum – which resounds with short bursts of staccato like tapping. Drumming is used for territorial displays between males. After hearing one, it just becomes a matter of scanning up and down a tree to locate the downy's presence.

Using its reinforced skull and chisel-like bill, the downy searches for insects behind bark and in snags. Beetles, ants, caterpillars, and assorted larvae comprise 75% of its diet. Downy woodpeckers are welcomed in orchards and provide pest control of the flat-headed apple tree borer. You may also see them at your feeder in the fall and late winter. They will eat a variety of birdseed and are easily attracted to suet feeders.

Downy woodpeckers search for mates and a suitable tree for nesting in late winter. Both male and female share in the parental duties, including excavating a nesting cavity, incubating the eggs, and raising the young.

Watch for the downy in the company of nuthatches and chickadees on your next hike, and listen for the genial sounds and friendly disposition of the midwest's smallest woodpecker.

Harvestmen Abound

Spiders and snakes, spiders and snakes. I'm going to learn to like 'em, no matter how long it takes. This simple rhyme rings true for many, as it takes time and the correct information to overcome our uneasiness for these creatures. One such creepy crawly that might need some insight is the harvestman, more commonly referred to as daddy longlegs. These eight-legged speedsters are technically not spiders. They belong in the same class **Arachnida**, with spiders, which also includes mites, scorpions, and ticks. That is where the similarities end. Spiders fall under the order *Araneae*, while harvestmen are in the order *Opiliones*, which have only one body part (true spiders have two), no venom, only two eyes rather than eight, and do not build a web.

Harvestmen get their name from the observation that they are more prevalent during harvest times in the fall. Daddy longlegs are active now in large numbers near protected areas, where they mate and lay their eggs, after which they will die by late fall when it becomes cold. During their life, harvestmen are found both indoors and out, on trees, grass, fence posts, and in fields. In the absence of being able to weave a web, harvestmen are created with speed and agility, able to track down and capture their prey. Their diet includes small insects, caterpillars, mites, and plant juices. A few larger spiders will prey on harvestmen, but birds, frogs, and toads generally keep their distance because of the foul odor released from behind the front legs, making for a distasteful meal. Additionally, harvestmen, when captured have the ability to drop off a leg to aid in their escape. The leg will not grow back but the daddy longlegs can survive without it.

Be careful not to confuse a harvestman with the long-bodied cellar spider, found in the corner of basements in the winter. Both have very long, thin legs, but cellar spiders hang upside down in an irregular web, which is the giveaway that they are not harvestmen. Daddy longlegs are great for overcoming a fear of spiders. Simply letting them run over your arm or leg on an autumn day, gives you the confidence that these giants of the insect world mean you no harm. In fact, they eat many of the spiders that build webs in our homes and rid our yards of other "pests." Collect a few during your next fall clean-up day and enjoy their splendid simplicity.

Standing on the Edge

Every so often, the call of the open road beckons and I succumb to the pursuit of wildness. The voice from nature - telling me to come and experience a few days alone, with only a map and a few essentials. Such was the case in late September. I heeded the call and left for an adventure in Michigan's Upper Peninsula.

My plan was to drive to Seney National Wildlife Refuge, observe the fall changes and witness the bird migration. From there, it would be strictly impulse. My drive to Seney was colored with sugar maples already starting to glow. Arriving as the sun set, I decided to camp under the stars just outside the refuge. The following morning I entered the refuge minutes before the sun welcomed me. Brilliant beams of ruby-red rose from the horizon and filtered through the clouds as I set off on an eight-mile hike. The refuge was set aside in 1935 for the protection of migratory birds. Over 95,000 acres comprised of forests, swamps, bogs, and marshes, provided the perfect setting to lose oneself and become absorbed in the landscape.

My hike was entertained with countless songbirds, numerous waterfowl, and an assortment of small mammals. I watched a beaver gnaw on speckled alder and darner dragonflies prowl the trail's edge for food. Each scenic vista, each set of tracks, and every call of nature, set my senses alight and stirred my soul.

Upon returning from my hike, and after a stop in the visitor center to explore the displays and chat with the volunteers, I left the refuge a bit tired from the walk and yet refreshed from my immersion into the wilderness. The journey continued east as I set forth to Whitefish Point. Along the way, I visited Tahquamenon Falls State Park. The U.P. is known for its waterfalls and Tahquamenon Falls tops the list (evidenced by a full parking lot on a Tuesday). The falls certainly did not disappoint, but the highlight for me was my reward for heading off the beaten track, or in this case, taking the trail less traveled. I came across the largest known white pine in the state park. It stood over 120 feet tall, approximately 175 years old and measured almost 5 feet in diameter. I let out an audible gasp when I witnessed the cathedral pine. Waterfalls are amazing, but this silent sentinel struck a chord with me. The tree is a timepiece, a testimony to vigilance, and reassurance that something so simple and true still exists.

My experience at Whitefish Point started at 5:30 am. I walked the beach and listened to the calm whispers of Lake Superior. Soon after, I met up with the resident birder/researcher from the observatory. Each morning a bird count is conducted, recording the number and species of birds coming across the bay and funneling south through Sault Saint Marie. Together we watched large numbers of redneck grebes, loons, blue-winged teals, and mergansers streak across the horizon. I was astounded at the distance in which the researcher could identify the waterfowl. The sheer numbers and speed of the birds also humbled me. It is wonderful to know that despite all of our progress, technology, and expansion, the magnitude of the fall migration and the resilience of nature, continue to resound in the hearts of people along its journey.

I met lots of different folks along my trip and I came to a few personal conclusions. We all need the presence of nature in our lives to provide a perspective and balance that cannot be found in the manufactured world. It is not enough to identify what we see in nature, but rather see relationships in our observations and make the connections of how it all fits together. And hopefully, we'll see ourselves in the mosaic.

To go out to walk silently in this woods – this
is a more important and significant means to
understanding…
I cannot have enough of the hours of silence when
nothing happens. When the clouds go by.
When the birds sing. When the trees say nothing.
I am completely addicted to the realization that
just being there is enough, and to add
something else is to mess it all up.

~ Thomas Merton

The Split Personality Tree

As I peered across one of the lakes
in the Nicolet National Forest, just miles
east of Eagle River, Wisconsin, I saw the shoreline aglow with
brilliant golden hues. I savored the moment; knowing that in a few
short weeks only the stark trunks and branches would remain to
shadow the landscape. I was witnessing, perhaps, one of the most
unique trees in the northwoods – the tamarack!

The tamarack, *Larix laricina,* is a coniferous tree (bearing cones
containing its seeds) that sheds all of its needles each fall. All
conifers, such as pines, spruces, and firs, lose needles, but only the
tamarack has a yearly shedding of *all* of its holdings. That makes
the tamarack a deciduous conifer.

Look closely at the braches of a tamarack. Small knobs protrude along the branches and during the spring and summer, contain 15-25 small needles. The needles are unusually soft and without the waxy protection found on firs and spruces. Tamaracks typically grow in bogs, along lakeshores, and open rocky sites. The shallow root system spreads outward, and with the help of fungi to transfer nutrients into their roots, the tamarack can survive the acidic conditions of swamps and bogs.

Some folks know this tree as the Eastern or American larch. They can grow up to 80 feet in height and live for over 200 years. Besides sprouting new trees from their roots, the tamarack produces mass quantities of cones every 3-6 years. During this period, a single tree can contain 20,000 cones and yield 5 million seeds per acre. This not only ensures new seedlings and a next generation, but invariably supports the small rodent population, which feed on the seeds. Voles, mice, shrews, chipmunks, and red squirrels, all eat conifer seeds. A healthy rodent population provides food for mammals and raptors. Badgers, bears, coyotes, fisher, hawks, and owls, (the list could go on and on) eat rodents as a part of their normal diet.

Who would have imagined the divinely distinct, yet profound influence the tamarack could have on the ecosystem? All this from a tree that enjoys the company of conifers, while acting like its deciduous aspen and birch friends.

Good Neighbor

I vividly recall the joy and excitement I felt upon landing at one of the many islands tucked away in the Boundary Waters Canoe Area in northern Minnesota. We had canoed for several hours and I was looking forward to setting up camp and basking in the peace and tranquility of solitude and isolation that the small islands afford. No sooner than the tent went up and fire wood gathered, the silence was broken and alarm sounded. A cry from above, like a ratcheting tool aimed straight at me; let us know we were not alone. For this island belonged to the red squirrel!

The red squirrel, *Tamiasciurus hudsonicus*, is a northwoods native, and along with the blue jay, is the alarm of the forest. But not just any alarm. It's a feisty, ruckus call that voices a warning to all and carries with it a commitment to defend its territory. Red squirrels live in coniferous and mixed hardwood forests and depend on the seeds of pine, spruce, and fir trees to survive. Their high-energy lifestyle and intense territorialism provide an entertaining backdrop when camping or hiking year-round.

Red squirrels spend their days gathering and storing food. Unlike gray squirrels that collect and bury individual acorns, red squirrels would just as soon bury the whole tree. Actually, they chew entire cones off from pine, spruce, and fir tree branches before they ripen and later retrieve them for storage. Cones are then deposited in tree cavities, hollow stumps, under logs, or anywhere they can be hidden. These food caches are the red's insurance needed to get through the coming winter. A red squirrel can eat over 100 cones a day, consuming the inner seeds and discarding the outer shells or shucks. Large midden piles of cone scales are easily found throughout the squirrel's range and can even be used to hide more food underneath.

Weighing only half a pound, red squirrels put on quite a show for their size. They will chirp and bark, flick their tail, and stamp their feet to warn off any perceived threat. Finally, with running speeds up to 15 miles an hour, they will chase off other squirrels, both reds and grays, until their territory and food are safe.

Besides conifer seeds, the red squirrel eats buds, berries, mushrooms, insects, and even birds' eggs and baby cottontails. Adults typically raise one litter a year, mating during winter, with 3 to 6 pups being born in late April. Young red squirrels are preyed upon by martins, owls, hawks, bobcats, foxes, and weasels.

Red squirrels are as much a part of the northwoods landscape as any white pine, loon, or beaver. Any camper or hiker will have stories to share about these red hot mammals and their hyper antics. I have come to look forward to their presence and learned to enjoy them as very interesting neighbors. Although, I'm not sure they feel the same way about me.

Friend or Foe?

Believe it or not, snakes are one of the top attractions at every zoo. The serpentarium, or snake house, is often the most visited exhibit each year. This tells us that we are naturally curious and most of us want to understand these creatures more. All snakes are

139

reptiles and have dry scaly skin, no eyelids or ear openings, and are carnivorous. Snakes are ectothermic (cold-blooded); hence, their body temperature is controlled by their surroundings. This explains much of their behavior. During hot summer days snakes will often stay underground or remain in dense vegetation to avoid overheating, and during cooler temps will bask on a rock to absorb the sun's heat.

In Wisconsin, there are 21 different types of snakes. One of the most common is the Western fox snake, sometimes called a pine snake. The fox snake is yellowish to olive gray in color, with large brown and black blotches along its back. The head is a rusty orange or dark copper, and the tail is pointed *without* a rattle. The fox snake is often misidentified as either a copperhead or rattlesnake because of its color, but like most snakes of Wisconsin, it is non-venomous and eats rodents, ground-nesting birds, and amphibians. The fox snake is a constrictor. It captures its prey in its jaws, then wraps tightly around the victim, preventing it from breathing, and swallows it whole.

Fox snakes are found in open habitats that include marshes, meadows, prairies, and fields. These snakes are active from April to October and then become dormant underground during the winter. Snakes are found where rodents are active. They help control the rodent population – beneficial for agricultural communities and keep diseases that rodents carry, such as hanta virus and Lyme's disease in check. Snakes also provide a food source for small mammals and birds. Hawks and owls feed regularly on snakes.

On your next visit to the countryside or to the zoo, stop and reflect on how these surreptitious predators fill their place in the ecosystem. The loss of prairie habitats is the greatest threat to maintaining snake populations. Only through education and recognizing their value in the environment can we continue to reap the benefits and enjoy these critters for generations to come.

Vacation Comes to the Northwoods

It has been a busy summer, the growing season is short. While we have been traveling, picnicking, and playing in the water, they have toiled under the sun, endured the wind, and held firm through the storms of the season. Now it is their turn. A vacation is due.

The leaves have thrown off the green uniforms of work. In their place, donned colorful gold, yellow, orange, and red frocks for travel. The work is complete, a job well done, another season in the books. It is time for a holiday.

The creatures of the north agree. The birds lock up the nest, meet companions for travel and head south. A tropical destination awaits. The frogs have been busy and labor towards their reward. A deep mud bath is the prescription. Their spa is the local ponds and wetlands as they sink into a winter paradise and forget the cares of the world. The bats are split as to their vacation. Some seek the comforts of a southern latitude, while others rest in the science of cryogenics, becoming one with their environment.

Some, like the bear live in the best of both worlds. A light slumber will do, and the joy of waking with precious cubs at her side is her bounty. The vacations have important roles and serve

141

the creatures well as we witness the divine grace and wisdom played out in nature.

So as we enter into the winter months, be grateful for the gray squirrels, chickadees, and snowshoe hares that stick it out with us. Their hearty nature and pioneer spirits are shared with the folks of the northwoods. Be gracious with the birdseed and fruit, (lest they be tempted to take their own vacation), and find joy in their presence as we sojourn on together.

We Come In Peace

Bats are truly unique mammals. There are 1,000 different species found in the world, and they exist in mountains, deserts, prairies, rain forests, wetlands, forests, and cities. In fact, bats can be found on every continent except Antarctica. Bats not only eat insects, but they pollinate flowers and distribute seeds. Some plants are pollinated exclusively by bats.

So why are they so misunderstood and feared? Myths, legends, and Hollywood movies have perpetuated misinformation to the public. We are now starting to understand the benefits of bats and people are welcoming bats into their community via bat houses and shelters (check out the Congress Ave. Bridge in Austin, TX).

In Wisconsin, bats are busy eating mosquitoes and moths during the evening hours. Some of these bats hibernate during the winter, while others migrate south. Here are a few bats in the area: *Little Brown Bat* – Small critter, about the size of a mouse. Very common throughout the state. They live in big colonies and will hibernate here in the winter. Will eat insects including flies, mosquitoes, and moths.

Big Brown Bat – Twice as big as the Little Brown Bat, this bat is common and likes to roost in attics, barns, garages, or simply on the side of a building. Likes to eat big, juicy beetles, cut worms, and rootworms, which help the farmers. Will also hibernate in the winter.

Eastern Pipistrelle – Very small, only 3 inches long, smallest bat in WI. It prefers to roost in caves, abandoned mines, and rock crevices and will hibernate in these caves in winter.

Indiana Bat – This bat is on the endangered species list. It forms huge colonies that number in the thousands. It also will feed on a variety of insects.

Silver-Haired Bat – This bat is smaller than the big brown bat. It is considered rare and lives a solitary life, roosting in trees in woodpecker holes and birds' nests. Interestingly it is the slowest flying bat in North America with speeds of 20-30 mph and will migrate south in the winter.

Red Bat – Another solitary bat, living in the forest, and will also migrate south in the winter. Bats usually just give birth to just one pup a year, but the red bat will give birth to twins each year. If a bat survives its first year, it has the potential to live for 30 years.

Keen's Bat – Very similar to the little brown bat, with longer ears. They roost in solitude, but will form colonial nurseries. They like to roost under the loose bark of trees.

Hoary Bat – The largest bat in our area. Has a grayish, yellow color and is found in the northern part of WI generally. Migrates south for the winter.

Fuzzy Forecaster

Turning on the nightly news and watching the weather segment always amazes me - with the latest technology like Doppler radar, satellite imagery, and computer simulated forecasts, today's meteorologist has more gadgets than a James Bond film. And all for what? To tell me there is 30% chance of rain. What ever happened to going outside and reading natures' clues for the upcoming weather? My guess is that we've become too sophisticated to rely on old stand-bys like, red sky at morning…, biting sand flies, and robins singing in the bush, all indicators of coming rain. There is even something to be said for grandpa's trick knee (joints often swell before a storm due to the drop in barometric pressure). On the other hand, maybe we have just not learned all the signs that present themselves. I am happy to report on a long-term forecaster found right the neighborhood – the woolly bear caterpillar.

The woolly bear caterpillar is a common sight in the fall, crossing sidewalks and roads in a hurry to get somewhere. It has a reddish-brown band in the center and jet-black fur on both ends. As a child I would often pick one up and watch as it curled itself into a protective ball. The woolly bear is actually the larvae, or worm stage, of the Isabella tiger moth. In the fall, the woolly bear caterpillar searches for a place to hibernate for the winter. In the spring, it emerges, feeds on any leafy vegetation, and then spins a cocoon. Several weeks later, the Isabella moth bursts forth in search of a mate to prepare the next generation of fuzzy forecasters.

Folklore says that the width of the inner, reddish-brown band determines the severity of the upcoming winter. A narrow band predicts a cold, hard winter, while a wide band indicates a mild winter. Several researchers have compared woolly bear bandwidths to actual winter records and found a surprisingly high percentage of accuracy in the predictions.

Truth-be-told, it might not look so good for a college-educated meteorologist to bring out a woolly bear on the six o'clock news. Then again, it may serve as a reminder that signs and answers are all around - if we are willing to let our sophistication go and embrace the simple revelations around us. As I plan for the upcoming winter season, I will look to nature's own "weather worm" as my guide.

Chirping Thermometer

With this autumn's run of warm weather, I have relished the cool nights as an opportunity to open the windows, air out, and enjoy the sounds of nature. Lately, I have been serenaded by nature's most familiar song: the chirp of the cricket.

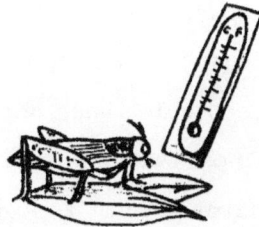

Crickets and warm nights go hand-in-hand and together are the perfect backdrop for fall camping. Crickets are also believed to be good luck. From England to the Far East, crickets were welcomed and even kept as pets. While I cannot vouch for the "pet" component of a cricket, I can recommend using them as nature's temperature gauge.

Male crickets, in an effort to attract a mate, rub their wings together (even though they do not fly) creating the chirping sounds we hear. Chirps are faster in warmer weather and slower when it cools. Count the number of chirps in 15 seconds, then add 37, and it will equal, or be very close to, the outside temperature. This equation applies to the common black field cricket, as there are other formulas for the tree cricket. So the next time it's too warm to sleep, open the window and you'll know just how warm it is. And no calculator needed!

The First Generation

Aspen are called pioneer species. What does the word "pioneer" bring to mind? Perhaps it's breaking new ground, the first to colonize, or a hearty spirit. Aspen trees, both big-toothed and quaking, are the most abundant trees in our area and the most wildly distributed trees in North America. Following a disturbance, such as logging, wind damage, or fire, aspens are typically the first trees to grow into the area. Once established, aspens send out root suckers that surface as new trees. Each new seedling is connected to the parent tree. Remarkably, a stand of aspen is actually one giant organism connected underground.

Since aspens are sun loving trees and shade intolerant, their seeds never get a chance to establish a second generation. Instead,

shade tolerant trees will succeed into the area and out compete the aspen. Look below the taller trees and see what is under them. This is called the understory. There may be small herbaceous plants or tree saplings. These may be the future of the forest.

During the fall, aspens turn a bright golden hue and provide a nice complement to the maples and oaks. Aspen is used for pulp in making paper, but its real value is to wildlife. Grouse will eat aspen buds, deer and snowshoe hares will dine on the leaves and twigs, beavers and porcupines will munch on the inner bark, and moose will eat it all. A thick stand of relatively young aspen is a wildlife magnet and great spot to explore during the fall and winter months.

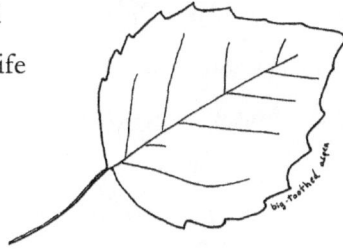

A Rose By Any Other Name

The sleek black glossy fur and white cap with two solid white racing stripes down its back, make the striped skunk the most easily identifiable mammal in the northwoods, and also puts it in contention for the most handsome. The striped skunk, *Mephitis mephitis,* well known to most, is commonly considered an odiferous creature not to be messed with. Getting past our sense of smell may open our eyes to seeing the skunk in a new light.

Striped skunks are nocturnal mammals that usually go unnoticed throughout our neighborhoods. The exceptions are when vehicles hit them and the pungent smell lingers for days or after the family dog lets its curiosity get the better of him or her. Skunks have two scent glands located on either side of the rectum, which are capable of discharging a malodorous fluid up to 15 feet in distance. Because of this powerful defense system, one might surmise that the skunk goes around randomly emitting its odor. Rather, as a result of its distinctive field marks, the skunk's coloration and means of protection are quickly associated and larger carnivores learn not to antagonize it. The one exception to this is the great horned owl. Great horns have little if any sense of smell and are the only natural predators skunks have.

Striped skunks are found throughout Wisconsin in habitats that include brushland, lightly wooded areas, grassy fields, pastures, woodpiles, and along lakes and streams with brushy boarders. It keeps a home range of ½ to 1 mile. The skunk has long, sharp claws on its forelimbs. For an animal about the size of a large housecat, its claws are impressive. The claws are used for digging in search of insects – mainly grasshoppers and crickets, but also large amounts of beetles, caterpillars, cutworms, and wasps. Skunks also eat mice, shrews, and moles, while 30% of their diet consists of plants, fruits, berries, and grains. Skunks also use their claws for digging out burrows along the sides of fields or brush patches. Burrows will average 20 feet long, usually 4 feet below the ground, and will house a female and 6 or 7 kits or a single male.

Skunks are very active during late spring, the summer months and into the fall. During the winter, male skunks can be active, while females and yearlings enter torpor until mating starts in February. As with most animals, the spring and fall are when the young ones are most susceptible to automobile hits. Upon encountering a skunk, I have found them to be shy, yet focused on their business at hand, and remarkably stunning in their coloration.

Farmers benefit from the skunk's healthy appetite for mice, rats, grasshoppers, squash bugs, and potato beetles. Homeowners will often find a family nesting under a deck or patio, and if they won't mind a couple weeks of walking a bit slower and trying not to frighten the visitors, the skunks will generally leave on their own. I hope that our noses will not dissuade our good sense. Imagine if skunks smelled like roses? They would then be everyone's favorite guests.

Fall Hunting

Nature walks are my favorite activity and regardless of how familiar I am with a trail, no two walks are ever the same. With binoculars and field guides in tow, I search out new discoveries. Lately, mushrooms have proven to be just the subject to enhance my wild walks.

Mushroom hunting has gone on since the beginning of time. Some are good to eat and many are *deadly poisonous*, but with such large varieties of shapes and colors, all make for interesting photography. With a little patience and a good field guide, the world of mushrooms can open right before you.

The mushrooms we see with our eyes are actually the fruit bodies of microscopic fungi, which grow underground or lie buried in trees or decaying materials. The visible fruit body is where the spores are stored and dispersed for reproduction. Fungi are responsible for breaking down plant matter in the process of decomposition.

Mushrooms are found during spring, summer, and fall - everything from the typical umbrella shaped ones on the ground and fan shaped conks growing from trees and stumps, to spikes, clubs, slimes, cups, and puffballs. One species that caught my attention this year is the colorful sulfur shelf mushroom.

Named for its blaze orange and yellow color, the sulfur shelf, *Laetiporus sulphureus,* is a bracket fungi, which fruits primarily on hardwood trees and stumps. The fan-shaped brackets grow up to 12" across and overlap with many layers. They often start off yellow and then turn bright orange with yellow margins. This past spring I noticed large numbers of sulfur shelf on oak stumps. This fall, I am seeing a new outbreak of these colorful conks, which goes by another common name – "chicken of the woods."

They are edible and considered "choice" by mushroom hunters. Gathering and preparing sulfur shelf takes perfect timing. I look for large ones, 8" wide and fleshy to the touch, and avoid ones that are old, tough, or wormy. Upon collecting a few large brackets, I wash them in cold salt water. This helps eliminate any bugs hidden within the folds. Then slice the conk into strips, dip in egg, roll in breadcrumbs or crackers, and deep fry on the stove, then serve warm with your favorite main dish. I noticed the texture is similar to chicken and the taste – super!

I would recommend that anyone interested in collecting mushrooms should first purchase, read, and study

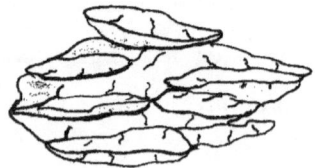

a field guide thoroughly. When in doubt, stick to photography – your collection will be a work of art!

Note: Sulfur shelf is widely regarded as a safe mushroom to eat for most people. While mushroom poisoning is unpleasant and can cause severe damage, and even death, knowledge and 100% positive identification will ensure this pastime does not become fatal. Also, because one person can eat a fungus with no ill effects, it is no guarantee that another can eat the same fungus without stomach upset or poisoning.

> And what is there to life, if a man cannot
> hear the lonely cry of the whippoorwill or the
> argument of the frogs around the pool at night?
>
> Attributed to Chief Seattle, 1856

Sounds of Silence

The afternoon had given way to the evening and the sun slowly descended upon the horizon, cradled by the waves before slipping out of sight. I was exploring the bluffs along Lake Superior where the Black River spills into the giant pool. Upstream from the river, tucked away from the trail, hid one of the many waterfalls the Upper Peninsula of Michigan lays claim to. The blaze red rays of the sun had skated through the white pines, hemlocks, and beech trees, glowing softly on the bark. As I walked to the waterfall, I listened to a red squirrel sharply announce its presence and heard chickadees keeping in touch with their flock thru the gentle *"de de de, de de de"* call. Then to my amazement, an ugly screeching of tires and loud engine roar broke the ambiance of the moment.

A car had left the tiny parking lot and the driver, for reasons unknown, needed to call attention to himself. What struck me was the incongruence of visiting such a scenic spot, enjoying the splendor, then leaving in a manner that defiles the peace of the place. I have always enjoyed nature for the opportunity to lose myself into the landscape, forget about the cares of the world and immerse into a habitat where I am not the focal point.

Unfortunately, some people cannot exist simply with nature. We see evidence of this on roadsides strewn with garbage, trails covered in litter, and rocks etched with initials and graffiti. But what about the noise? The clamor of our culture can defile the landscape as much as any debris can. Is it possible to experience nature without the sounds of society ringing in the ears?

Taught from an early age to make noise, the familiar cry of "let your voice be heard" resounds from every corner. Louder stereos, bigger televisions, cell phones, pagers, ipods, and computers, all ensure that our culture's grasp is never out of reach. Cars, planes, snowmobiles, boats, ATV's and jet skies, take us places we otherwise could never go, and in doing so, pollute the airwaves with rumbling fumes and an unnatural racket. Some folks have bought into this ideology, disguised as technological advancement, and actually fear the sounds of silence. I however, grow weary of the constant din of traffic, lawnmowers, radios, and small talk, and seek to hear the whispers of the wild.

Anyone who has gone camping, visited a state park, or traveled to a wilderness area, such as the Boundary Waters Canoe Area in northern Minnesota, know that to be free from the hum of progress is easier said than done. Airplanes are probably the biggest offender in breaking the silence, followed closely by ATV's. Sit in the middle of a state forest somewhere and you will likely hear the distant dirge of highway traffic or construction machinery. Pure silence does not exist, for even nature has a voice, but the large tracts of unbroken wilderness are the closest we can come to finding it.

The sounds of nature lend themselves to an increased awareness of our surroundings. The light call of the chickadee, the gentle scamper of the field mouse, the turning of aspen leaves, and swaying of branches, appeal to our senses and develop the tools for understanding the rhythms of the wild. We can distinguish between the trot of a fox and the browse of a deer. We will know the rustle of grouse and the scurry of the squirrel. And in turn, we will hear the quiet voice inside telling us to simplify and let go of the bonds that encumber our lives. I will continue to seek out the subtle sounds of silence, free from our culture's call, and enjoy the therapy of nature's timeless talk.

Let the fields be jubilant, and everything in them.

Then all the trees of the forest will sing for joy.

Psalm 96:12

NOTES

APPENDIX: Mammal Files

Badger, *Taxidea taxus*   34 teeth
Habitat: Open grasslands, sandy soils, open woodlots.
Food: Small rodents, reptiles, amphibians, and insects.
Range: Varied, utilizes many dens.
Mating: Aug./Sept.
Gestation: D.I. 240 days, implantation occurs in Feb./March
Litter: 2-3 born in April/May
Predators: None
Important rodent predator, chiefly nocturnal.

Little Brown Bat, *Myotis lucifungus*   38 teeth
Habitat: Open forests near lakes and wetlands for feeding.
Food: Moths, mosquitoes, mayflies, midges, beetles.
Range: 1-5 miles
Mating: Aug./Sept.
Gestation: D.I., implantation occurs the following spring, actual 50-60 days.
Litter: 1 born in June.
Predators: Owls, hawks, snakes, skunks, raccoons, martens.
Life span up to 33 years, roosts in tree cavities, caves, brush, crevices.

Beaver, *Castor canadensis*   20 teeth
Habitat: Small lakes, ponds, streams, near aspen, birch, and willow thickets.
Food: Water lilies, arrowheads, cattails, grass, bark, twigs, leaves of aspen and
birch.
Range: 10-20 acres, less than 6 miles.
Mating: late Jan./Feb.
Gestation: 120 days.
Litter: 2-4 born in May.
Predators: Wolves, fox, mink.
Largest rodent in N. America, fueled fur trade, grows continually, keystone
species.

Black bear, *Ursus americanus*   42 teeth
Habitat: Mixed forest, thick understory w/den sites and clearings.
Food: Berries, acorns, roots, leaves, buds, insects, grubs, fish, frogs, eggs, small
mammals.
Range: adult males 8-25 sq. miles.
Mating: late June/July.
Gestation: D.I. 225 days, 100 actual.
Litter: 2-3 cubs born in late Jan./Feb.
Predators: None. Wolves and male black bears may take young cubs.
Enter a winter torpor in late Oct./Nov. In fall spend 20 hrs a day eating.

Bobcat, *Lynx rufus*   28 teeth
Habitat: Forests with wet areas.
Food: Small mammals, birds, hares, rabbits.
Range: 25 miles, usually 2-3 sq. miles.
Mating: Feb./March
Gestation: 62 days.
Litter: 2-4 born in April/May
Predators: Few if any, great horned owl may take young.
Solitary and inconspicuous mammal, will use varied habitat.

Chipmunk, *Tamias striatus*   20 teeth
Habitat: Mature, open hardwood forests, edges, logs, stumps, rocks.
Food: Acorns, beechnuts, maple keys, berries, cherries, mushrooms, insects.
Range: ¼ to 1 acre.
Mating: April
Gestation: 30 days.
Litter: 4-7 born in May.
Predators: Hawks, fox, wolves, weasels, snakes.
Anti-social, winter hibernators, defends its burrow aggressively. Have cheek pouches.

Coyote, *Canis latrans*   42 teeth
Habitat: Forest edges, meadows, swamps, prairies, open woodland.
Food: Mice, voles, hares, rabbits, squirrels, birds, eggs, insects, grass, berries.
Range: 5-25 sq. miles, more often 2-3 sq. miles.
Mating: Feb.
Gestation: 60 days.
Litter: 4-8 pups born in April.
Predators: Wolves, bears.
Extremely adaptable to habitats and human expansion.

Deer mouse, *Peromyscus maniculatus*   16 teeth
Habitat: Mature forests, richer soils, but common in all woodlands.
Food: Seeds, conifer and maple, berries, nuts, flowers, beetles, snails, bugs, spiders.
Range: 1/10 – 1/3 of an acre.
Mating: Variable, Feb.-Nov.
Gestation: 22 days.
Litter: 3-6 per litter, 2-5 litters per year.
Predators: Owls, snakes, weasels, fox, coyotes, martens, raccoons, skunks, etc.
Most common mouse of northwoods, important disperser of seeds, populations rise and fall w/ tree seed cycles.

Eastern cottontail, *Sylvilagus floridanus*   28 teeth
Habitat: Heavy brush, forests w/openings, swamp edges, weed patches.
Food: Green vegetation, twigs, and bark.
Range: 3-20 acres.
Mating: March-May.
Gestation: 30 days.
Litter: 4-6 per litter, 2-4 litters per year.
Predators: Lynx, bobcats, owls.
Crepuscular, important game mammal, garden pest.

Ermine, short-tail weasel, *Mustela erminea*   34 teeth
Habitat: Northern forests, open country, bushy areas, close to water.
Food: Voles, mice, chipmunks, rabbits, birds, snakes, frogs, insects.
Range: 30-40 acres.
Mating: July.
Gestation: D.I. nine months.
Litter: 4-9 born in April.
Predators: Owls, hawks, ox.
Turn snow white during winter, dependent on day length.

Fisher, *Martes pennanti*   38 teeth
Habitat: Mixed hardwood forests, cutover wilderness areas.
Food: Small mammals, martens, porcupines, birds, fruits, ferns.
Range: 10 sq. miles.
Mating: April.
Gestation: D.I. 352 days.
Litter: 1-4 born in April.
Predators: None. Once thought to eat fish, hence the name, but does not. Only
real predator of porkies.

Gray fox, *Urocyon cinereoargenteus*   42 teeth
Habitat: Wooded areas, heavy brush, close to water.
Food: Cottontails, rodents, fruits, insects.
Range: 1-2 sq. miles.
Mating: Late Feb.-March.
Gestation: 51-61 days.
Litter: 3-7 pups born in April-May.
Predators: Coyotes, fisher, wolverine.
Climbs trees for refuge and for prey.

Red fox, *Vulpes vulpes*   42 teeth
Habitat: Semi-open country, forests, varied.
Food: Squirrels, rabbits, hares, mice, voles, birds, snakes, turtles, frogs.
Range: 1-2 sq. miles.
Mating: Jan/Feb.
Gestation: 53 days.
Litter: 3-6 born in Mar./April.
Predators: Coyote, fisher. Skillful hunter, nocturnal, elusive, has harsh bark.

157

Snowshoe hare, *Lepus americanus*   28 teeth
Habitat: Swamps, forests, thickets.
Food: Succulent vegetation, twigs, barks, buds, some meat.
Range: 10 acres.
Mating: Late March – August.
Gestation: 36 days.
Litter: 2-4 per litter, 2-3 litters a year.
Predators: Lynx, bobcat, barred owl, great horned owl, great gray owl.
Solitary, does not build nest, populations fluctuate every 6-10 years.

Lynx, *Lynx canadensis*   28 teeth
Habitat: Boreal forests, mixed coniferous forests.
Food: Snowshoe hares, grouse, red squirrels.
Range: Up to 50 miles.
Mating: Jan./Feb.
Gestation: 62 days.
Litter: 1-4 born in Mar./April.
Predators: None.
Solitary, reclusive hunter, major influence on hare populations.

Marten, *Martes americana*   38 teeth
Habitat: Fir, spruce, hemlock forests, also cedar swamps.
Food: Red squirrels, rodents, insects, birds, fruits, nuts.
Range: 1 sq. mile.
Mating: July.
Gestation: D.I. 270 days, implants in mid-winter.
Litter: 2-4 born in April/May.
Predators: Fishers, coyotes, wolves, owls.
Reintroduced to Nicolet National Forest, still protected status. Curious.

Mink, *Mustela vison*   34 teeth
Habitat: Dens in bank burrows, along streams and lakes.
Food: Small mammals, muskrats, eggs, fish, crayfish, birds, reptiles, amphibians.
Range: 2-3 miles.
Mating: Feb./March.
Gestation: D.I. 51 days.
Litter: 3-6 born in Apr/May.
Predators: Wolves, fox, bear, bobcats, great horned owls, snowy owls.
Fur prized, ferocious killer of muskrats, intense musk glands, name is Swedish for stinky animal.

Moose, *Alces alces*   32 teeth
Habitat: Forests with broadleaf trees, mixed conifer stands, wetlands, meadows, bog.
Food: Aquatic plants, broadleaves, ferns, buds, twigs.
Range: 8-16 sq. miles.
Mating: Sept.-Oct.
Gestation: 240 days.
Litter: 1 or 2, born in May.
Predators: Wolves or bear may take a calf.
Icon of the northwoods, they can weigh 1,000 lbs. and stand 7 ft. at shoulders.

Muskrat, *Ondatra zibethca*   16 teeth
Habitat: Marshes, pond edges, slow moving streams, open water, cattails.
Food: Aquatic vegetation, clams, frogs, fish, corn.
Range: Several acres.
Mating: Mar./Apr., again through August.
Gestation: 22-30 days.
Litter: 4-8 per litter, 2-3 litters per year.
Predators: Mink, red fox, raccoons.
Readily observed mammal, important furbearers, and effective burrowers.

Otter, *Lutra canadensis*   36 teeth
Habitat: Old lodges along stream and lakes, dense thickets of willow and alder.
Food: Fish, crayfish, muskrats, insects, mice, aquatic vegetation.
Range: 15 miles.
Mating: March/April.
Gestation: D.I. 12 months.
Litter: 2-4 born in April/May.
Predators: Wolves, coyotes, bobcats.
Luxurious fur, tough, impervious to weather, playful.

Porcupine, *Erethizon dorsatum*   20 teeth
Habitat: Forested areas, boreal forests.
Food: Bark, inner bark, woody and herbaceous vegetation.
Range: 75-375 acres.
Mating: Oct./Nov.
Gestation: 210 days.
Litter: 1 born in Apr./May.
Predators: Fisher, bobcat, coyote.
Slow solitary mammal that uses smell and touch.

Raccoon, *Procyon lotor*   40 teeth
Habitat: Near streams and lakes, bordering wooded areas, all states.
Food: Crayfish, amphibians, eggs, reptiles, larvae, berries, acorns, nuts.
Range: 1 to 2 miles.
Mating: Feb./March
Gestation: 64 days.
Litter: 3-5 born in Apr./May.
Predators: Coyotes, wolves, fisher, owls, eagles.
Dens in hollow tree or ground burrow, does not hibernate.

Short tail shrew, *Blarina brevicauda*   32 teeth
Habitat: Forests, grasslands, marshes, brush areas.
Food: Insects, worms, snails, plants.
Range: 1 acre.
Mating: March-May, Aug.-Sept.
Gestation: 17-21 days.
Litter: 5-8 per litter, 2-4 litter per year.
Predators: Raptors, coyotes, foxes, martens.
Shrew's salivary glands produce poison which can kill a mouse or vole.

Striped skunk, *Mephitis mephitis*   34 teeth
Habitat: Forest edges, shorelines, thick brush, rocky field edges, crop fields.
Food: Insects, grasshoppers, beetles, crickets, cutworms, eggs, reptiles, nuts,
berries, roots.
Range: 10 acres.
Mating: Late Feb./March
Gestation: 63 days.
Litter: 5-7 born in May.
Predators: Great horned owls.
Generalist, important rodent controller, enters winter torpor when below 15°F.

Eastern Gray Squirrel, *Sciurus carolinensis*   22 teeth
Habitat: Hardwood forests w/oak trees, river bottoms.
Food: Nuts, seeds, fungi, fruits, cambium layer of trees.
Range: 2-7 acres.
Mating: Jan./Feb.
Gestation: 44 days.
Litter: 2-4 per litter, 2 litters per year, 2nd in Aug.
Predators: Hawks, owls, coyotes.
Diurnal mammals, active mornings, late afternoons, lives in drays, leaf nests, or
cavities.

Red Squirrel, *Tamiasciurus hudsonicus*   20 teeth
Habitat: Pine and spruce, mixed hardwood forests, swamps, red pine stands.
Food: Seeds, nuts, eggs, fungi, conifer cones.
Range: 1 acre.
Mating: Feb./March
Gestation: 38 days.
Litter: 2-7 per litter, 2 litters per year, 2nd in Aug./Sept.
Predators: Hawks, owls, martens, fishers, minks, weasels, fox, coyotes, bobcats.
Gregarious and very territorial, high energy. Good wildlife watching.

Meadow vole, *Microtus pennsylvanicus*   16 teeth
Habitat: Open habitat with dense grass cover, low, moist areas, near streams or woods.
Food: Grasses, sedges, seeds, grains, bark, insects.
Range: 1 acre.
Mating: Throughout year.
Gestation: 21 days.
Litter: 5-6, up to 11, several litters per year.
Predators: Fox, coyotes, martens, raptors, etc.
Prolific rodent, uses sun as compass, less active on moonlit nights.

Whitetail deer, *Odocoileus virginianus*   32 teeth
Habitat: Mixed and deciduous forests, clearings, brushy areas, swamps, young stands.
Food: Grass, sedges, clover, flowers, bud, shoots of maple, aspen, birch, acorns, cedar, yew.
Range: 1 sq. mile.
Mating: November.
Gestation: 200 days.
Litter: 1-2 born in May.
Predators: Wolves, coyotes, bears.
Currently abundant, important game mammal, popular wildlife watching.

Gray wolf, *Canis lupus*   42 teeth.
Habitat: Wilderness forest, tundra, unbroken tracts of land, beaver meadows.
Food: Deer, beaver, snowshoe hare.
Range: 40 sq. miles.
Mating: Feb./March.
Gestation: 63 days.
Litter: 4-10 born in April/May.
Predators: None, raptors and bears may take a pup.
Intense social structure. An adult wolf will eat approx. 20 deer a year.

Index

www.ingramcontent.com/pod-product-compliance
Lightning Source LLC
Chambersburg PA
CBHW030015290326
41934CB00005B/352